Gallery
of
American

Quilts

1849-1988

American Quilter's Society

P.O. Box 3290
Paducah, KY 42002-3290

Notice

The quilts in this book are no longer for sale. They were offered by the members of the American Quilter's Society in 1987 and early 1988. Approximately 75% of these quilts were sold. The unsold quilts were returned to the members.

The price of a full year's subscription (4 issues) of the *Quilts For Sale Catalog* is $14.00. Each catalog contains 100 full-color quilts for sale, a description and price. For the latest copy send $4.00 to:

> *Quilts for Sale Catalog*
> c/o American Quilter's Society
> P.O. Box 3290
> Paducah, KY 42002-3290

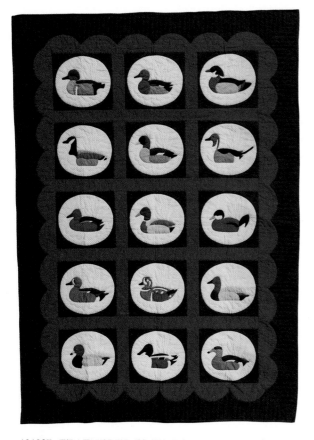

101387 - FEATHERED FRIENDS; 66″ x 95″; earth tones; cotton & cotton blends; made in 1986 in Kentucky; hand appliqued, hand quilted. This quilt displays 15 different ducks and geese in true-to-life colors. The ducks are enhanced by sashings and borders in earthtone shades. $920.00

201387 - THE TULIPS ARE COMING, THE TULIPS ARE COMING; 85″ x 105″; 2 shades of rose, green & off-white; 100% cotton; made in 1986 in Wisconsin; hand appliqued, hand quilted. $549.00

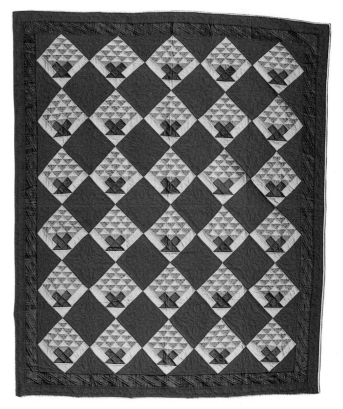

301387 - BLOOMING TULIP BASKETS; 88″ x 108″; blue/off-white/dark red tulips; 100% cotton; made in 1986 in Wisconsin; hand appliqued, machine pieced, hand quilted. $549.00

401387 - BASKET; 84″ x 98″; shades of green, red & yellow; cotton & polyester blend with Dacron blend; made in 1984 in Illinois; machine pieced, hand quilted; traditional basket quilt. $374.00

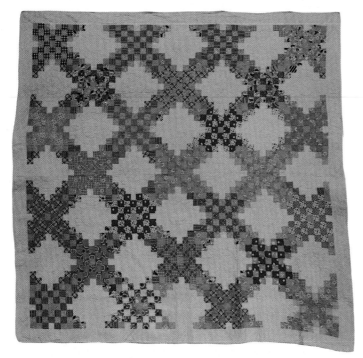

102387 - IRISH CHAIN; 84″ sq.; multicolor; cotton; made c. 1930 in Pennsylvania; machine pieced, hand quilted; multitude of different colored calicos, hand appliqued, excellent condition. $190.00

202387 - LEMOYNE STAR; 78″ x 81″; blue, red & white; cotton; made in 1935 in Pennsylvania; machine pieced, hand quilted; excellent condition. $265.00

302287 - CHURN DASH; 70″ sq.; cotton; made c. 1900 in Pennsylvania; hand pieced, hand quilted; multicolor prints with yellow calico, quilted 16 st./in.; mint condition. $345.00

402387 - FLOWERING LOVE APPLE; 69″ x 73″; green, red, peach & white; all cotton; made in 1910 in Pennsylvania; hand appliqued, hand quilted; original pattern, 14 stitches per inch, good condition. $340.00

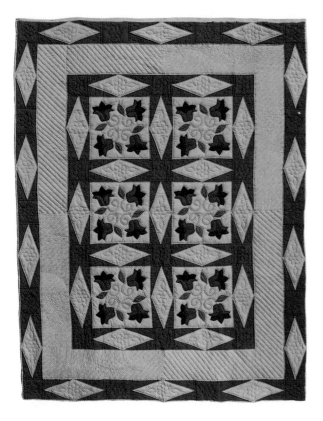

103387 - TULIP APPLIQUE; 82″ x 104″; rose & maroon on off-white; cotton & polyester blend with Dacron batting; made in 1985 in Illinois; machine pieced, machine appliqued, hand quilted. **$432.00**

203387 - AMERICAN BEAUTY ROSE; 87″ x 104″; shades of red with olive green on white; cotton & polyester blend with Dacron batting; made in 1983 in Illinois; machine pieced, hand quilted; machine appliqued with machine embroidery. **$432.00**

303387 - LILY; 82″ x 98″; orange & green on white; cotton and polyester blend with Dacron batting; made in 1983 in Illinois; machine pieced, hand quilted. **$374.00**

403387 - PANSY; 72″ x 85″; multicolor; cotton; made in early 1900's, quilted in 1986; hand pieced, hand quilted; pansies are hand appliqued & pieced, different colors, peach sash, cotton top, poly batting, unbleached muslin back; has age spots. **$196.00**

104387 - SQUARE IN A SQUARE - a scrap quilt; 67″ x 84″; bright colors; cotton-polyester batting, cotton lining; made in 1977 in Illinois; machine pieced, hand quilted; quilted by the piece. **$230.00**

204387 - PINWHEEL with Ice Cream Cone Border; 70″ x 92″; multicolor blocks set with blue; made in 1975 in Illinois; hand pieced, hand quilted; there are two (2) quilts alike — mirror images — intended for use on twin beds, bright pinwheel blocks set with blue & lined with same blue, nice quilting. Buy one or both. **$374.00 each**

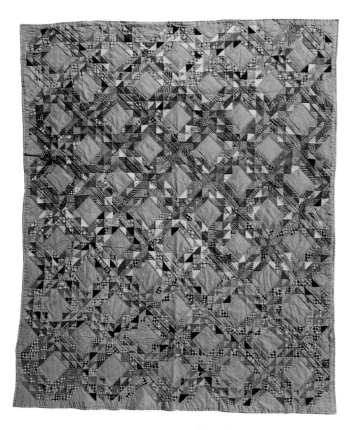

304387 - OCEAN WAVES; 76″ x 88″; hand pieced, hand quilted; lovely old top-newly quilted by Amish in Indiana, collection of scraps of homespun around lavendar; check center block; lavendar backing. **$455.00**

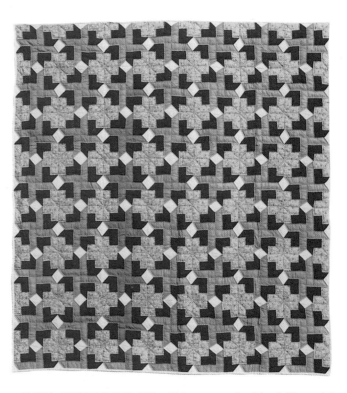

404387 - WHIRLYGIG; 74″ x 80″; green, red, white & blue print; hand pieced, hand quilted; old design; graphic; newly quilted. **$340.00**

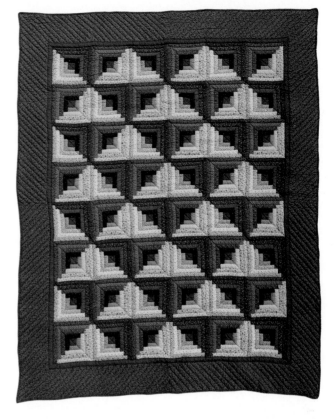

105387 - PAINTED POPPIES; 78″ x 88″; pink, green & white; cotton & cotton-polyester blends; made in 1986 in California; hand appliqued, hand quilted; pink & burgundy poppies hand appliqued on white background, variation of Stearns & Foster pattern, polyester batting & plenty of close hand quilting.
$949.00

205387 - LOG CABIN; 75″ x 96″; blue with rust; cotton & polyester; made in 1986 in Illinois; machine pieced, hand quilted; beautiful blend of 17 fabrics make up the color scheme of this quilt.
$375.00

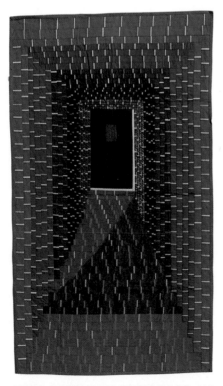

305387 - BLUE HALL/PLUM DOOR; 40″ x 80″; blues, rusty red, plum; 100% cotton; made in 1984 in Massachusetts; machine pieced, machine quilted; this quilt was made in one section in a variation of the Log Cabin technique. The image depicts a search for the way into a new phase of life.
$1,081.00

405387 - TEAL/MAHOGANY; 43″ x 73″; teal, mahogany, turquoise; 100% cotton; made in 1985 in Massachusetts; machine pieced, machine quilted; this quilt is part of a series of quilts made with an image of a jar or lantern. This "jar" is full of energetic pink & yellow flashes.
$1,277.00

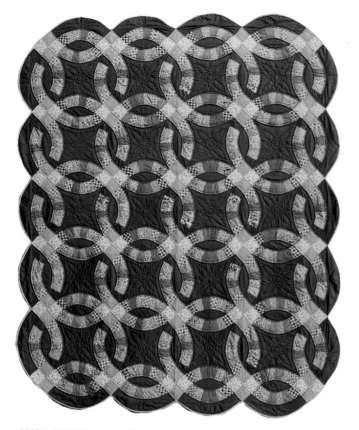

106387 - WEDDING RING; 80″ x 97″; hand pieced, hand quilted; blue polished cotton background, yellow binding, 1920's prints, newly quilted. **$685.25**

206387 - DARK MEDALLION; 68″ x 78″; hand pieced, hand quilted; beautiful collection of fabrics in late 1800's, top newly quilted (dated in feather border 1985). **$518.00**

306387 - LONE STAR; 80″ sq.; claret & white; cotton; made in 1910 in Pennsylvania; hand pieced, hand quilted; claret calicos & black sprigged white calicos, classic design, 14 st./in., good condition. **$334.00**

406387 - EVENING STAR; 64″ x 81″; multicolored; all cotton; made in 1930 in West Virginia; hand pieced, hand quilted; each star uses different fabrics; good condition. **$276.00**

107387 - DAHLIA; 95″ x 110″; mauve with off-white background; cotton, cotton/poly; made in 1986 in Missouri; machine pieced, hand quilted; Dacron batting, 8-9 st./in. $391.00

207387 - AMERICAN EAGLE; 76″ x 76″; blue, red, yellow on off-white; 100% cotton; made in 1930's; hand pieced, hand quilted; part of estate settlement, apparently never used, some very light stains on top, beautiful workmanship. $288.00

307387 - "RICHMOND"; 73″ x 92″; cotton; made in 1930 in Pennsylvania; machine pieced, hand quilted; uncommon pattern made of multicolored cotton prints, 12 st./in., good condition. $213.00

407387 - FRIENDSHIP QUILT; 85″ x 85″; blue, white & multicolored; all cotton; made in 1930 in West Virginia; machine pieced, hand quilted; attractively embroidered by various makers who have each signed their own block, excellent condition. $460.00

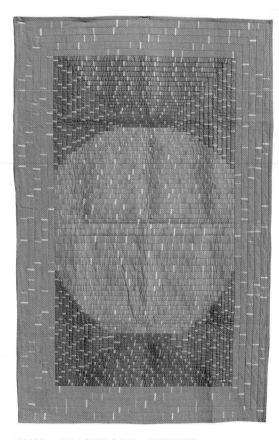

108387 - PEACH/ROSE/LAVENDER; 40″ x 66″; peach, rose, lavender-grey; 100% cotton; made in 1985 in Massachusetts; machine pieced, machine quilted; last of a series of quilts made with an image of a jar or lantern. The "jar" appears to be situated in the space behind the peach frame. **$1,173.00**

208387 - KALAUNA ME KA MAILE - Crown & maile leaves; 71″ x 102″; rust & gold; Imperial Broadcloth 50/50 cotton & polyester, backing is Cranston V.I.P. calico, Mountain Mist polyester batting; made in 1985 in Marshall Islands; hand appliqued, hand quilted; original design based on old traditional Hawaiian theme. **$552.00**

308387 - WINDBLOWN TULIPS; 82″ x 82″; white with blues & green appliques; cottons; made in 1985 in California; hand appliqued, hand quilted; appliqued tulips & leaves in a circular effect. Original border design by quilter's husband. **$633.00**

408387 - VARIATION FLYING GEESE - RAINBOW; 78″ x 95″; cotton; made in 1985 in California; hand pieced, hand quilted; navy background & backing. **$575.00**

109387 - LONE STAR; 92″ x 105″; rust & brown; polyester & cotton; made in 1986 in Missouri; hand & machine pieced, hand quilted; bonded polyester fill, quilted by the piece.   **$374.00**

209387 - MICHIGAN STAR; 99″ x 102″; rust & brown; polyester & cotton; made in 1986; hand & machine pieced, hand quilted; bonded extra plump fill.   **$403.00**

309387 - LOG CABIN; 102″ x 105″; light to dark; cotton, some cotton blends with polyester; made in 1981 in Alabama; machine pieced, hand quilted; double batting, brown broadcloth backing. **$552.00**

409387 - MARTHA WASHINGTON FLOWER GARDEN; 100″ x 102″; blue center with coordinated colors; all cotton; made in 1986 in Alabama; hand pieced, hand quilted; double batting with white sheet backing, double quilting, set together with white blocks.   **$690.00**

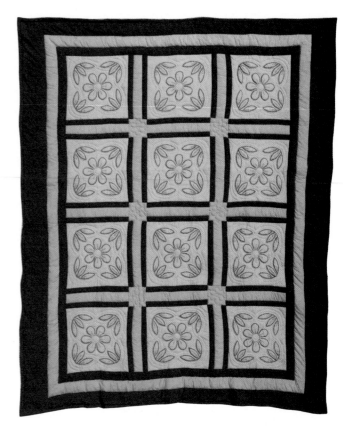

110387 - LONE STAR; 72″ x 84″; greens, rose & yellow; cotton; made in 1966 in Idaho; machine pieced, hand quilted; star variegated cotton prints & solids, yellow background, rose border, yellow back, never used. **$230.00**

210387 - NO NAME; 88″ x 107″; white/pink/burgundy; broadcloth with 2 lb. Dacron batting; made in 1986 in Idaho; machine pieced, hand quilted; cross-stitched daisies on white blocks, pink & burgundy stripping & border, reversible, pink back. **$460.00**

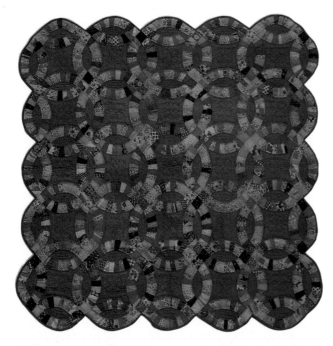

310387 - WEDDING RING; 78″ x 78″; blue background with multicolored hues; cotton fabrics with Mountain Mist polyester backing; made in 1930's in Indiana; hand pieced, hand quilted; has a fine collection of 1930's prints which are beautifully set against the blue background. **$340.00**

410387 - OCEAN WAVES; 83″ x 89″; blue/white; cottons (shirt fabrics) with Mountain Mist polyester batting; top made in 1920's in Indiana; hand pieced, hand quilted; great collection of old shirt fabrics gives this quilt a very soft look. **$345.00**

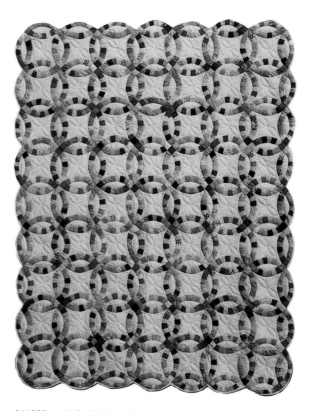

111387 - LOG CABIN; 75″ x 99″; cotton & polyester; made in 1985; machine pieced, hand quilted; rose Log Cabin has extra plump bonded polyester fill; pillow shams to match.
$288.00

211387 - DOUBLE WEDDING RING; 83″ x 104″; multicolored with white fill; cotton/polyester; made in 1986 in Missouri; machine pieced, hand quilted; extra plump Du-Pont Dacron polyester batting. **$345.00**

311387 - GRANDMOTHER'S FAN; 70″ x 80″; mixed colors; made in 1985 in Tennessee; hand pieced. **$219.00**

411387 - DECEMBER MORN; 95″ x 106″; white & blue with peach; cotton/polyester; made in 1986 in Missouri; hand & machine pieced, hand quilted; has DuPont Dacron Hollofil polyester batting. **$374.00**

14

112387 - EMBROIDERY DAHLIA; 98″ x 98″; wine on ecru; cotton; made in 1986 in Illinois; hand embroidery, machine pieced, hand quilted; put together with tiny dots on wine. $276.00

212387 - FLOWER GARDEN; 102″ x 104″; multicolored with mint green & ecru; cotton; made in 1986 in Illinois; machine pieced, hand quilted. $276.00

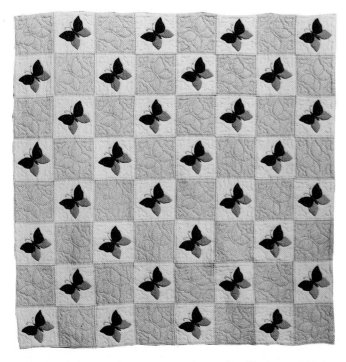

312387 - BUTTERFLY; 100″ x 100″; brown & gold on ecru; cotton; made in 1986 in Illinois; hand pieced, hand quilted; brown & gold butterfly appliqued on ecru, set with brown & ecru blocks, butterfly outlined with black embroidery. $276.00

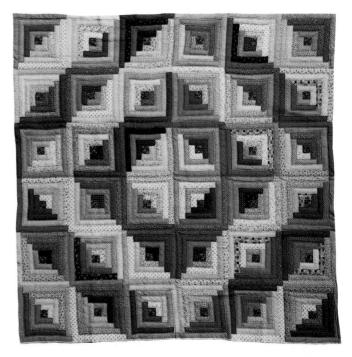

412387 - LOG CABIN; 99″ x 101″; earth tones; all cotton; made in 1986 in Alabama; machine pieced, hand quilted; ecru broadcloth backing, double polyester batting. $673.00

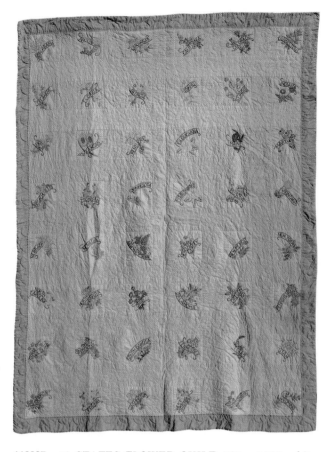

113387 - 48 STATES FLOWER QUILT; 78″ x 106″; white beautifully embroidered blocks with pale green back; cotton; made in 1957 in Illinois; hand embroidered, machine pieced, hand quilted; some stains. **$328.00**

213387 - CORNER STONE LOG CABIN; 102″ x 102″; shades of brown & tan; cotton; made in 1986 in Illinois; machine pieced, hand quilted; corner of orange & brown. **$253.00**

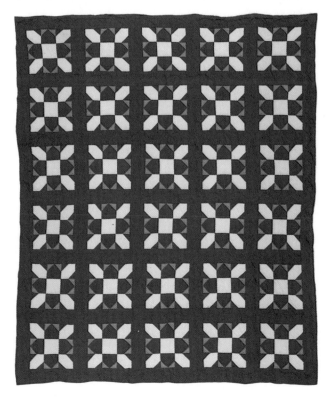

313387 - PRAIRIE FLOWER; 85″ x 100″; burgundy & pink print; cotton; made in 1985 in Illinois; machine pieced, hand quilted. **$288.00**

413387 - FAN; 100″ x 100″; shades of blue on white; cotton; made in 1986 in Illinois; machine pieced, hand quilted; light & dark shades of blue set on white. **$253.00**

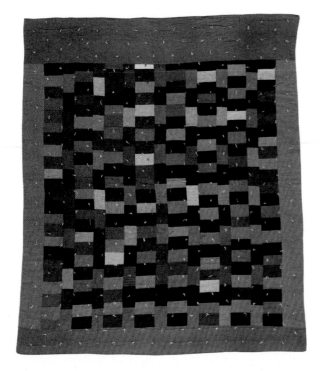

114387 - ANTIQUE COMFORTER; 72″ x 86″; dark woolen blocks on front with grey speckled flannel back; made in 1930 in Illinois; hand tied; tied with pink yarn, some stains on back.
$489.00

214387 - AMERICAN SAMPLER; 96″ x 112″; olives & blues; white percale; made in 1975 in Illinois; cross-stitched, hand embroidered, machine pieced, hand quilted.
$374.00

314387 - PUSSY WILLOW/LILAC WREATH; 88″ x 106″; orchid, green & white; made in 1986 in Illinois; machine pieced, hand quilted; embroidered blocks set together in lilac & white with purple & white points.
$374.00

414387 - TULIP RHAPSODY; 89″ x 106″; pale blue & white with red tulips; made in 1985 in Illinois; hand embroidered, machine pieced, hand quilted; embroidered red tulip blocks set together with robin egg blue; blue & white points.
$374.00

115387 - PYRAMID; 80″ x 110″; multicolored; cotton & cotton polyester; made in 1985 in Arkansas; machine pieced, hand quilted; washable fabrics, solids & prints. **$202.00**

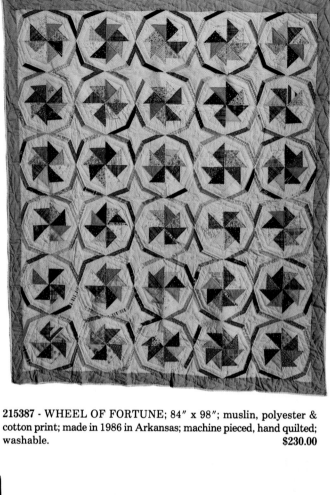

215387 - WHEEL OF FORTUNE; 84″ x 98″; muslin, polyester & cotton print; made in 1986 in Arkansas; machine pieced, hand quilted; washable. **$230.00**

315387 - TUMBLER; 92″ x 103″; brightly colored scraps with navy border; cotton; made in 1986 in Arkansas; machine pieced, hand quilted; hand quilted heart on border. **$345.00**

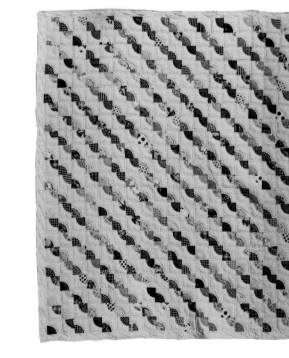

415387 - FALLING TIMBERS; 85″ x 96″; unbleached muslin all colored scraps; cotton & unbleached muslin; made in 1986 in Ark.; hand pieced, hand quilted; yellow border. **$299.00**

116387 - HEARTS; 72″ x 88″; pale blue with blue floral back; cottons; made in 1980 in California; hand quilted; counterpane or white-on-white whole cloth with 2″ white eyelet edging. **$259.00**

216387 - LITTLE SCHOOLHOUSE; 63″ x 79″; muslin - primaries & lavender; 100% preshrunk cotton; made in 1986 in New Jersey; machine pieced, hand quilted; bright houses on a muslin background, tulips & garden fence quilted around border, red calico backing, no marks. **$403.00**

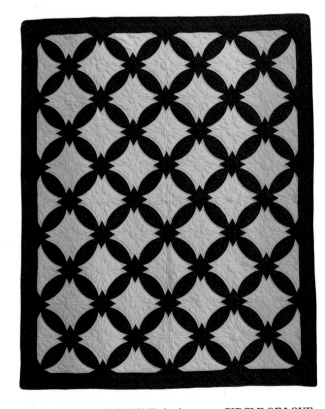

316387 - WINNER'S CIRCLE also known as **CIRCLE OF LOVE;** 72″ x 88″; brown/peach flowers and off-white; 100% cotton; made in 1984 in Wisconsin; hand pieced, hand quilted. **$345.00**

416387 - DELECTABLE MOUNTAIN MEDALLION; 84″ x 101″; rose with blues & whites; made in 1986 in Wisconsin; hand & machine pieced, hand quilted; medallion of four delectable mountain patches set on point in a field of background fabric, flying geese border, finished with variable stars in corners. **$374.00**

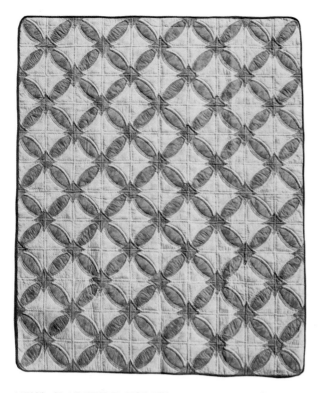

117387 - CLARKE'S FAVORITE; 77″ x 95″; apricot & cream; cotton; made in 1972 in California; hand pieced, Amish hand quilted. **$397.00**

217387 - STAR AND CROSS; 75″ x 94″; navy & white; cotton; made in 1984 in California; Amish quilting. **$403.00**

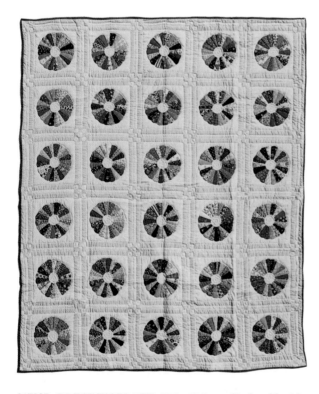

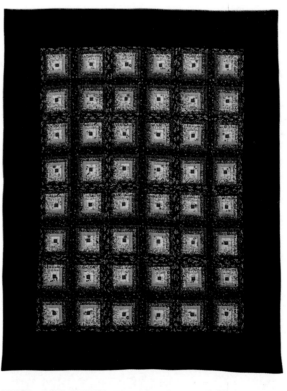

317387 - DRESDEN PLATE; 77″ x 93″; muslin & gold with rust back; cotton; made in 1975 in California; hand pieced, hand quilted. **$397.00**

417387 - LOG CABIN; 76″ x 94″; browns & blues; cotton; made in 1982 in California; hand pieced, hand quilted; quilting "in the ditch" carries pattern to the back, pleasing shade of blue for back of quilt. **$403.00**

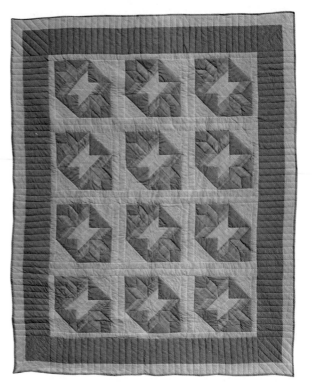

118387 - TUMBLIN' STAR; 100″ x 102″; blue on blue; all cotton; made in 1986; machine pieced, hand quilted; two poly batting in quilt, quilting on both sides of seam. $564.00

218387 - QUEEN CHARLOTTE'S CROWN; 78″ x 96″; white, orchid plaid & orchid solid; cotton poly; made in 1986 in Missouri; machine pieced, hand quilted; top pieced with orchid plaid, orchid solids & white, lining orchid; could be used as reversible quilt. $374.00

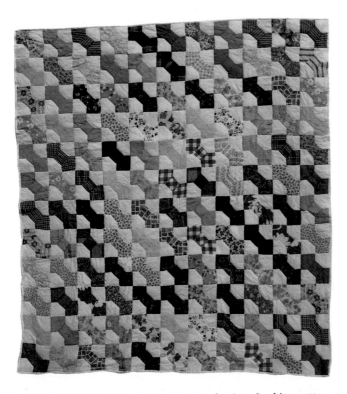

318387 - BOW TIE; 87″ x 96″; variegated prints & white; cotton, poly; made in 1986 in Missouri; machine pieced, hand quilted; white lining. $317.00

418387 - CRAZY QUILT PATTERN; 72″ x 83″; browns, tans, grays & heather tones; polyester, wool & corduroy; made in 1986 in Michigan; machine pieced; all washable fabrics with polyester batting. $173.00

119387 - STARS OVER FLORIDA; 79″ x 97″; browns, beiges, all autumn colors; all cotton & polyester; made in 1986; machine pieced, hand tied; double Mountain Mist polyester batting, beige backing, all washable. $288.00

219387 - TRIP AROUND THE WORLD; 80″ x 92″; red & white; cotton & polyester blends; made in 1986 in Kentucky; hand pieced, machine quilted; bright colors of various reds & white, white lining, polyester padding, machine washable. $317.00

319387 - COAL MINERS; 68″ x 80″; red & white, blue denim; cottons & denim; made in 1985; machine pieced, machine quilted; can be used as wallhanging, coverlet or quilt; white lining polyester padding, machine washable. $202.00

419387 - BUTTERFLY PATTERN; 111″ x 110″; polyester & cotton blend; made in 1986 in Arkansas; hand appliqued, hand quilted; 100% bonded polyester batting. $518.00

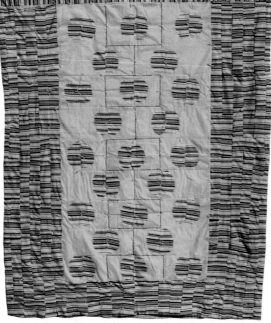

120387 - ORNAMENTS; 78″ x 91″; blue, gold & white striped balls, machine appliqued on muslin; cotton, cotton blends; made in 1986 in Arizona; machine appliqued, hand tied; extra soft polyester batting, muslin backed. **$230.00**

220387 - NO NAME; 70″ x 80″; blue, orange & green print laced together with muslin; made in 1930's in Arizona; hand pieced, hand quilted; some stains. **$288.00**

320387 - STARS & SQUARES; 85″ x 97″; green squares, multicolored stars; cotton, cotton blends; made in 1986 in Arizona; hand pieced, hand quilted; extra soft batting, muslin backed. **$545.00**

420387 - NO NAME BABY QUILT; 45″ x 60″; red & white; cotton, cotton blends; made in 1986 in Arizona; machine pieced, hand quilted; washboard pattern with extra soft polyester batting, muslin backed. **$98.00**

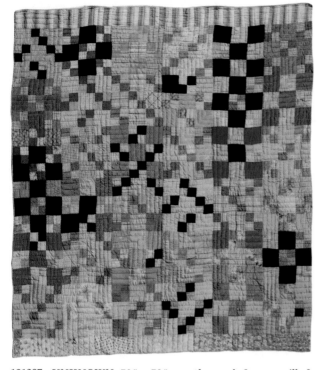

121387 - UNKNOWN; 70″ x 79″; mostly peach & navy; silk & silk like materials; made in Arkansas; machine pieced, hand quilted; bought at a yard sale, estimated to be at least 50 years old.   **$150.00**

221387 - GRANDMOTHER'S FLOWER GARDEN; 76″ x 94″; peach with various colors; poly & cotton blends; made in 1985 in Kentucky; hand pieced, hand quilted; made of various colors of rosettes outlined with peach; light peach lining, scalloped sides.   **$317.00**

321387 - DANISH HEARTS; 40″ x 40″; red & white; 100% cotton; made in 1986 in California; machine pieced, hand quilted; 5 red & white pieced hearts set diagonally, heart echo quilting.   **$144.00**

421387 - AGAPE-S; 31″ x 31″; black, gold & ming green; cotton, polished cotton, cotton decorator fabric; made in 1985 in Tennessee; hand appliqued, hand quilted; heart represents love God has given mankind, the flowers represent the beauty of nature, the honeycomb quilting lines represent law & order of the universe.   **$288.00**

124387 - DOLPHINS & WAVES; 26″ square; white on ocean blue; cotton, poly blends; made in 1986 in Hawaii; hand appliqued, hand quilted; original pattern celebrates the playful dolphins who inhabit the island waters. **$115.00**

224387 - IPU KUKUI; 25½″ square; deep rose on off-white; poly cotton blends; made in 1986 in Hawaii; hand appliqued, hand quilted; pattern by Poakalani. The "Kukui" or "Coconut" tree, played an important role in the Hawaiian Islands and was a source of food, gourds & oil for lamps. **$100.00**

324387 - TREE OF PARADISE WALL QUILT; 27½″ x 27½″; tiny blue scrap triangles with blue borders; cotton & cotton poly blend; made in 1982 in California; hand pieced, hand quilted. **$60.00**

424387 - IRISH CHAIN; 45″ x 57″; beige with rust & grey; poly/cotton blend; made in 1986 in North Dakota; machine pieced, machine quilted; subdued earth tones; appropriate as an afghan, quilt, wallhanging or large crib quilt. **$75.00**

125387 - BABY ANIMALS; 42″ x 42″; lavender; polyester & cotton; made in 1986 in Missouri; hand painted, hand quilted; polyester bonded fill. **$45.00**

225387 - "KE PE'AHI ME KA LEI" Royal Fan & Wreath; 42″ x 54″; turquoise blue with light blue background; Imperial Broadcloth 50/50 cotton & polyester; backing is Cranston V.I.P. calico; Mountain Mist polyester batting; made in 1986 in Marshall Islands; hand appliqued, hand quilted; original design based on Hawaiian tradition. **$449.00**

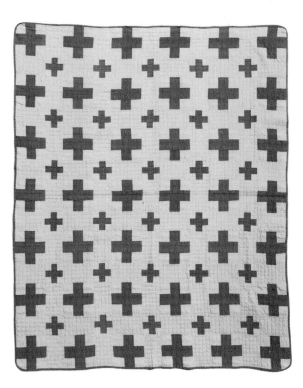

325387 - CLOWN BABY QUILT; 36″ x 46″; yellow, blue & red on white background; cotton/polyester; made in 1986 in Missouri; hand & machine pieced, hand quilted; hand embroidered, points are yellow, blue, red & striped, same as colors used on clown & bloomers; lining is white with yellow dots. **$55.00**

425387 - RED CROSS QUILT; 67″ x 81″; red & white; cotton; made in Illinois; hand pieced, hand quilted; quilted in 1918 from scraps from the workroom of the Red Cross Centralia Chapter Hdqtrs., Chicago, IL. The reason for the Chapter was to make night shirts for the servicemen overseas. **$1,150.00**

126387 - LONE STAR; 51½" x 51½"; tan, rust & green; 100% cotton; made in 1986 in New Jersey; machine pieced, hand quilted; wallhanging has sleeve on back, all fabrics preshrunk; backing is tan print; no marks; signed.   **$213.00**

226387 - APPLE TREE; 45" x 61"; green & blue; cotton & blends; made in 1986 in New Jersey; machine pieced, hand quilted; fun child's quilt or wallhanging, "apples" can be "picked", velcro attached, machine appliqued; backing is a green print high lift batting; no marks.   **$98.00**

326387 - CRYSTAL STARS; 46" x 47"; blues & beiges; cottons & cotton/poly blends; made in 1984 in California; hand & machine pieced, hand quilted; original design made in a Nancy Donahue class.   **$184.00**

426387 - TRIP AROUND THE WORLD; 68" x 78"; pastels; polyester; made in 1985 in Kentucky; hand pieced, hand quilted; made of soft pastel of polyester, very pretty & decorative for girls room; durable.   **$202.00**

101687 - BASKET; 66″ x 72″; multicolor feedsack prints & periwinkle; cotton; made c. 1930 in Pennsylvania; hand quilted 12 st./in. Good condition but there's a small age stain on bottom edge. **$311.00**

201687 - BOW TIE; 70″ x 71″; blue & white; cotton; traditional pattern in an unusual set; made c. 1915 in Pennsylvania; hand pieced and densely hand quilted 14 st./in. The half border is a "deliberate" mistake. Good condition. **$374.00**

301687 - LONE STAR; 84″ x 94″; poly-cotton; different shades of blue, mostly hand pieced and hand quilted, some machine piecing **$288.00**

401687 - LANCASTER; 100″ x 105″; blue; cross-stitched, hand pieced, hand quilted; double border design parades rows of florals across an eggshell percale top; cross-stitched in tones of blue. **$460.00**

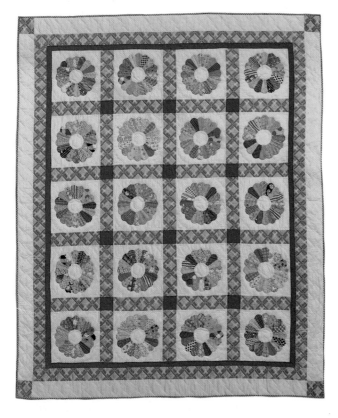

102687 - "DRESDEN PLATE"; 71″ x 85″; cotton; made in 1930 in Pennsylvania; machine pieced, hand appliqued; multicolor calicos & rose; machine pieced, hand appliqued & hand quilted 12 st./in. Mint condition.   **$276.00**

202687 - CAKE STAND; 75″ x 84″; yellow & white; cotton; made c. 1920 in Pennsylvania; machine pieced, hand quilted 16 st./in. in feather wreaths & cross hatch. Very good condition but has two faint stains.   **$334.00**

302687 - DRESDEN PLATE; 82″ x 100″; red & pastels on muslin; old pieces but newly assembled and quilted; Indiana.   **$518.00**

402687 - FLOWER GARDEN; 64″ x 79″; all prints from 1920's; green backing; Indiana.   **$403.00**

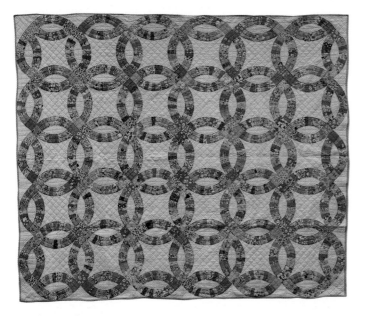

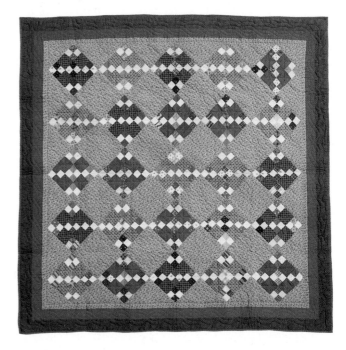

103687 - WEDDING RING; 90″ x 74″; pastels from 1920's quilted in green; Indiana. $328.00

203687 - "SINGLE CHAIN"; 76″ x 76″; gray and red with browns; old top, newly quilted; Indiana. $317.00

303687 - MONKEY WRENCH; 63″ x 76″; deep tones, old pieces, newly assembled; Indiana. $374.00

403687 - CRAZY QUILT; 62″ x 83″; multi-color, primarily red; velvet, satin, satin ribbon, cotton backing; made c. 1880 in Michigan; hand pieced, hand quilted; immaculate condition. It has much embroidery (designs and around pieces). Some painted pieces. "Turkey" red backing. $575.00

104687 - LOVERS KNOT; 70″ x 70″; pumpkin & white; cotton; made in 1940's in Tennessee; machine pieced, hand quilted; summer quilt, maple leaf quilting.   **$144.00**

204687 - SUNBURST (or SIXTEEN POINT STAR); 82″ x 72″; blues on cream; 100% cotton; made in 1984 in California; machine pieced, hand quilted; quilted by group in California. Beautiful wreath quilting between stars.   **$489.00**

304687 - CAPITAL T; 68″ x 88″; dark brown & light blue; 100% cottons; made in 1984 in Massachusetts; machine pieced, hand quilted; this quilt is quilted in the ditch (seam line) & has a cream print backing.   **$368.00**

404687 - BUCKEYE BEAUTY; 82″ x 97″; brown tones; cotton blends; made in 1986 in Utah; machine pieced, hand quilted; contains over 25 new, pre-washed fabrics. Fairfield bonded batting.   **$317.00**

105687 · APPLIQUED HEARTS AND OHIO STAR; 94″ x 94″; off-white, red, green & aqua blue; 100% cotton, cotton-polyester blends; made in 1987 in Minnesota; machine pieced, hand quilted, hand appliqued; made of new material with flannel on back for extra warmth. Dacron-polyester Mountain Mist batting.   **$575.00**

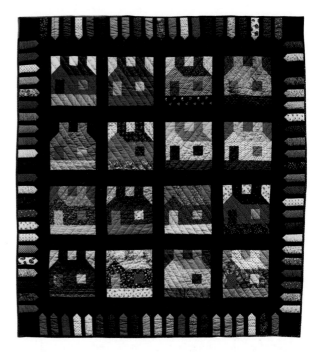

205687 · WILD & WOOLEY HOUSE QUILT; 70″ x 77″; black with printed scraps; 100% cotton; made in 1985 in Wisconsin; machine pieced, hand quilted; a quilt made just for the fun of it by a prize-winning quilter. Small calico backing. Pictured in *Quilter's Newsletter* # 179, page 45. **$805.00**

305687 · BROKEN STAR; 84″ x 97″; rust on off-white background; cotton & cotton-polyester blends; made in 1986 in California; machine pieced, hand quilted; 1½″ diamonds make this quilt; small stars in the corners, plenty of quilting with feather circles in white squares and calicos on borders.   **$863.00**

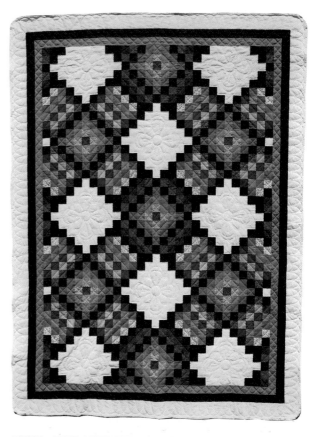

405687 · PHILADELPHIA PAVEMENT; 73″ x 97″; white with greens, blues & rose; 100% cotton, polyester batt-ultralight; made in 1987 in Minnesota; machine pieced, hand quilted; 989 patchwork squares in shades of green, blue & rose alternating with off-white. Diagonal quilting with floral design in white blocks, scalloped stitching on border.   **$460.00**

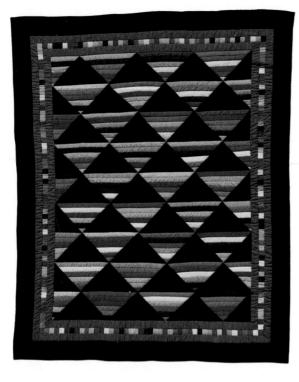

106687 - "AMISH SPARKLE"; 53″ x 64″; 100% cotton; made in 1986 in Wisconsin; machine pieced, hand quilted; Amish-type wallhanging made with black and sparkling solid colors. **$269.00**

206687 - LOG CABIN; 94″ x 113″; green & beige; polyester cotton; made in Illinois; machine pieced, hand quilted; new quilt. **$345.00**

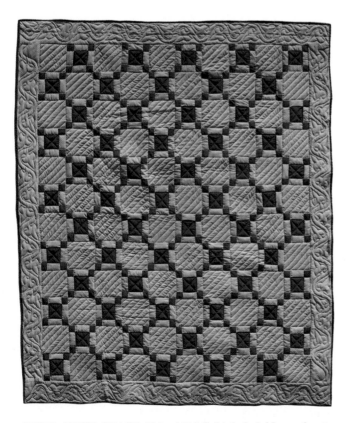

306687 - IRISH CHAIN; 92″ x 108″; light & dark blue; polyester cotton; made in Illinois; machine pieced, hand quilted; new quilt. **$345.00**

406687 - LOG CABIN; 99″ x 119″; rose & blue; polyester cotton; made in 1986 in Illinois; machine pieced, hand quilted; new quilt. **$345.00**

107687 - DOUBLE WEDDING RING WITH BORDER; 85″ x 102″; brown & rust; 100% cotton top, seamless 100% cotton lining, polyester batting; made in 1986 in Tennessee; machine pieced, hand quilted; all fabrics pre-washed. Received 2nd place at Parsons, TN, Quilt Show.
$460.00

207687 - "ESTHER'S FANTASTIC SWIRL"; 82″ x 92″; shades of brown & beige with blue accents; cotton, poly-cotton blends, poly batting, cotton backing; made in 1986 in Indiana; hand & machine pieced, hand quilted; original design using fan pattern, took Best of Show at Brown County, IN, Fair.
$489.00

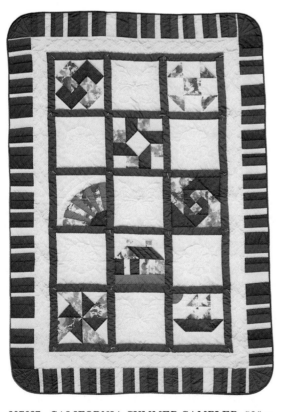

307687 - CALIFORNIA SUMMER SAMPLER; 58″ x 84″; bright blues, greens, orange/white; cotton/cotton-blend; made in 1984 in California; machine pieced, hand quilted; this is done in the glorious colors of California. The traditional patterns in the squares were chosen for how they remind the quiltmaker of this area. **$288.00**

407687 - "PUA KALIKIMAKA" (CHRISTMAS FLOWER); 42″ x 68″; green & red on pale ice green background; 50/50 polyester-cotton Imperial Broadcloth; backing is VIP 100% cotton calico; made in 1986 in Marshall Islands; hand pieced, hand quilted. **$598.00**

109687 - STAR FLOWER; 52″ x 52″; dusty roses, off-white & with touches of satin & lace; cotton & blends; made in 1985 in California; machine pieced, hand quilted; this is LOG CABIN arranged to form the star flower. **$173.00**

209687 - A CHILD'S SAMPLER; 31″ x 46″; pastel blue, pink, green & lavender; cotton & poly-cotton; made in 1985 in New Mexico; hand & machine pieced, hand quilted; this quilt may be machine washed in the delicate cycle & damp dried in the dryer. **$144.00**

309687 - MANY STARS; 25″ x 34″; browns, rust & tans; cotton, cotton blends, poly batting; made in 1982 in Minnesota; machine pieced, hand quilted; an experiment with six different star patterns. **$75.00**

409687 - CONCENTRIC TRIANGLES #1; 40″ x 40″ hexagon; brown, tan & beige; cottons & blends; made in 1986 in New Jersey; machine pieced, hand quilted. **$202.00**

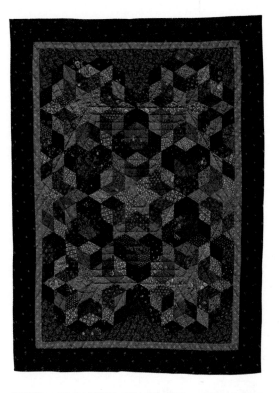

110687 - CONCENTRIC TRIANGLES #2; 45″ x 56″; beige & tan; cottons & blends; made in 1986 in New Jersey; machine pieced, hand quilted.   **$202.00**

210687 - FLOATING STARS; 32″ x 42″; black & burgundy; cottons & blends; made in 1986 in New Jersey; machine pieced, hand quilted.   **$202.00**

310687 - INNER CITY VARIATION; 33″ x 43″; rich browns, blues & rust; cottons & blends; made in 1983 in Arizona; a wallhanging with a three dimensional feel. Hand pieced, except for the border. Blocks appliqued to the rust background; hand quilted.   **$403.00**

410687 - NOSEGAY; 33″ x 40″; white with pastel flowers; 100% cotton & voile; made in 1986 in New York; hand pieced, hand quilted; polyester fill; signed & dated.   **$115.00**

112687 - LEMOYNE STAR; 36″ x 49″; brown, yellow, green & red; cottons, cotton blend woven plaids, cotton batting; made in 1986 in Maine; machine pieced, hand quilted; child size or wallhanging, quilted in the ditch with 7-8 st./in. $230.00

212687 - MISSOURI PUZZLE; 43″ x 43″; black & white; cotton polyester; made in 1985 in Missouri; machine pieced, hand quilted; pieced in solid black, black print & white lining. $87.00

312687 - "KUUIPO"; 30″ x 30″; clay (burgundy shade) on white; poly-cotton blends; made in 1987 in Hawaii; hand appliqued, hand quilted; "Kuuipo" is "sweetheart" in Hawaiian, echo quilting surrounds the design, two border strips frame the wallhanging. $144.00

412687 - "HIBISCUS"; 24″ x 24″; gold on white; cotton-poly blends; made in Hawaii; hand appliqued, hand quilted; the pattern depicts one of the most popular flowers in Hawaii. $92.00

113687 - ''FRIEZE''; 30″ x 32″; light blue & natural; cotton/polyester; made in 1987 in Maryland; hand quilted; light blue background & border with mitered corners. $173.00

213687 - NIGHT LIGHTS (Traditional Name: SHADOWS); 52″ x 52″; navy, black, red, orange, burgundy, yellow, blue & aqua; nearly all cottons, a few poly-cottons, all prints; made in 1983 in Australia; machine pieced, hand quilted. $230.00

313687 - CHECKERBOARD PATTERN; 60″ x 80″; kelly green & white; cotton & cotton blend; made in 1986 in Ohio; machine pieced, hand quilted; tiny, even hand stitching in cable pattern. $184.00

413687 - LOG CABIN; 76″ x 89″; poly-cotton & perma-press muslin; made in 1986 in Illinois; machine pieced, hand quilted; beige prints with muslin in center of block. $317.00

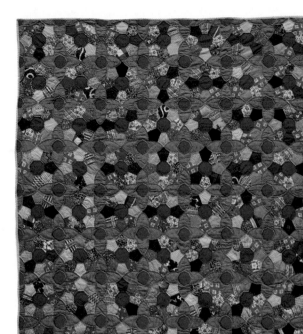

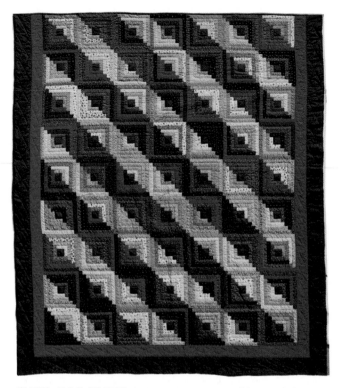

114687 - "FLOWER TYPE"; 68″ x 77″; green, yellow, red & multi-print; cotton; made in 1982 in Tennessee; hand pieced, hand quilted; 2 designs are seen - a Flower Garden & Dresden Plate. **$115.00**

214687 - LOG CABIN; 95″ x 110″; cream, gold, rust & brown; calico, cotton & polyester; made in 1979 in California; hand pieced, hand quilted; tones of cream & golds in diagonal stripe pattern with rust & brown diagonal stripe. **$518.00**

314687 - DELECTABLE MOUNTAIN; 72″ x 85″; red & white; polyester & cotton; made in 1982; hand pieced, hand quilted; this was patterned after a winner in the 1933 Chicago World's Fair. **$403.00**

414687 - RAIL FENCE; 80″ x 96″; browns; cotton; made in 1984 in California; hand pieced; the narrower pieces allow better shading of colors used; hand quilted by an Amish quilter. **$403.00**

115687 - FEED SACK QUILT; 85″ x 98″; multi-color; all cotton feed sacks; made in 1940 in Arkansas; machine pieced, hand quilted; this quilt is made from all cotton feed sacks, both top and backing; hand quilted. **$230.00**

215687 - HEXAGON STAR; 84″ x 118″; navy, red muslin; cotton & cotton polyester; made in 1986 in Arkansas & Colorado; hand & machine pieced, hand quilted; the quilt from which this pattern was taken was made in the late 1800's, though there is a difference in the way this one is set together. **$230.00**

315687 - MEANDERINGS; 80″ x 80″; navy, forest green, brick red & putty; cottons & poly/cottons, American & Australian; made in 1985 in Maryland; hand & machine pieced, hand quilted; center medallion adapted from *It's O.K. If You Sit On My Quilt* book. **$690.00**

415687 - DOUBLE IRISH CHAIN; 78″ x 88″; grey, pink & white; 100% cotton (all fabric including backing); made in 1986 in Massachusetts; hand pieced, hand quilted; this quilt in pinks & greys features a quilted floral pattern with hearts & feathers on the border. **$460.00**

40

116687 - LOG CABIN - BROKEN; 72″ x 88″; pink, burgundy, cream brown; cotton & cotton-poly combo; made in 1985 in New York; machine pieced, machine quilted; this quilt was quick-quilted on the sewing machine, machine washable & dryable.
$230.00

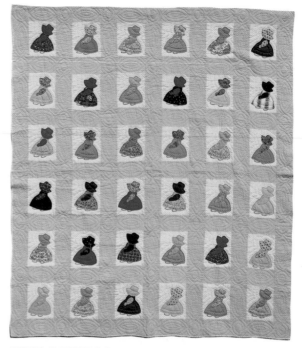

216687 - DUTCH DOLL; 84″ x 98″; green trim with white blocks; cotton & double knit; made in 1982 in Kentucky; hand pieced, hand quilted; gingham & double knit dresses put together on white blocks & green trim. $115.00

316687 - MIDNIGHT TULIPS; 82″ x 96″; black & red; gingham & cotton; made in 1986 in Kentucky; hand pieced, hand quilted; gingham tulips, appliqued on diamond black blocks, white briar stitch around each block, red gingham trim. $403.00

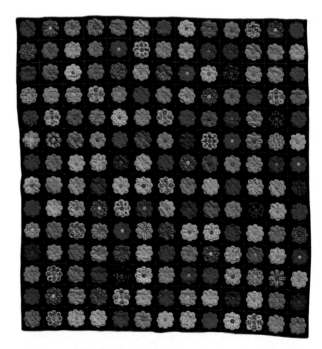

416687 - "MIDNIGHT FLOWERS"; 86″ x 91″; black blocks with all colors of flowers; cotton; made in 1986 in Kentucky; hand pieced, hand quilted; gingham flowers, appliqued on 6½″ x 6½″ black blocks with white briar stitch around blocks.
$403.00

117687 - CROSS-STITCH TULIPS; 78″ x 93″; royal blue, white & lavender; cotton & cotton blends, poly batting; made in 1984 in Minnesota; machine pieced, hand quilted; cross-stitched squares are from a kit; 24 tulips blocks, large scalloped border on three sides. A tulip design is quilted in sash & border. **$547.00**

217687 - FLOWER BASKETS; 72″ x 88″; pale yellow background with brown & rust; cottons, poly batting (Fairfield Needle Punch); made in 1985 in Minnesota; machine pieced, hand quilted, hand appliqued; twelve basket blocks set on points are pieced in brown & yellow with a gold applique bow on the handles. Quilting is braid & flowers. **$547.00**

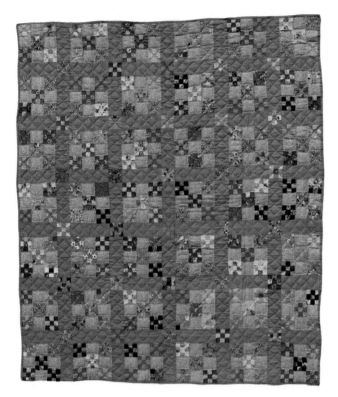

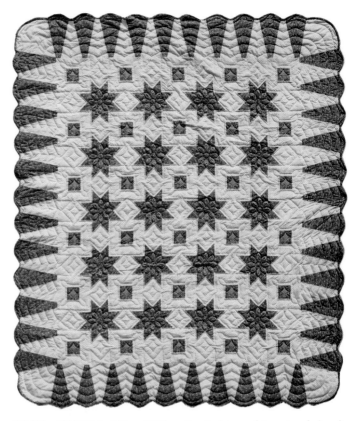

317687 - NINE PATCH; 78″ x 88″; cotton; hand pieced, hand quilted; old top hand pieced 1920-30, hand quilted in 1986 with feed sack back. Dusty blue background, multi-colored patches, Dacron batting, made in Missouri. **$196.00**

417687 - DAHLIA; 96″ x 110″; cotton/poly; machine pieced, hand quilted; dusty blue with gold & aqua butterflies, poly/cotton top & off-white back. Dacron batting, made in Missouri in 1987. **$380.00**

118687 - DRUNKARD'S PATH; 82″ x 67″; cotton with cotton batt; made in 1977 in West Virginia; hand pieced, hand quilted; pink with pink & green print. $202.00

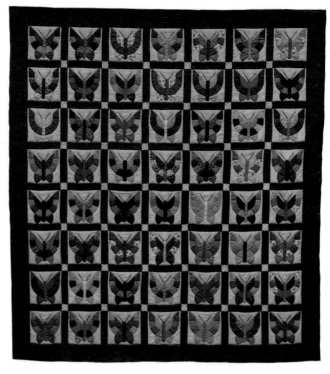

218687 - BUTTERFLIES; 97″ x 88″; green; cottons & blends; made in 1986 in West Virginia; hand pieced, hand quilted; multi-colored butterflies on pale green with dark green sashing. $345.00

318687 - LOVESICK GOOSE; 106″ x 108″; white goose on green poly-cotton; trigger (poly-cotton blend) lining weaver; made in 1987 in Arkansas; hand pieced, hand quilted; king size polyester & cotton blend with poly-fil batting. $575.00

418687 - SPRINGTIME IN ARKANSAS; 112″ x 118″; applique on cream trigger, orange & brown striped; trigger (cotton & poly top); made in 1986 in Arkansas; hand pieced, hand quilted; quilt is large king size, could be used for spread without dust ruffle; poly-fil batting. $799.00

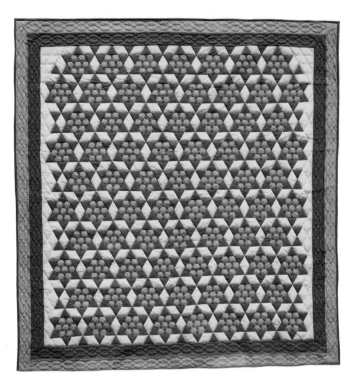

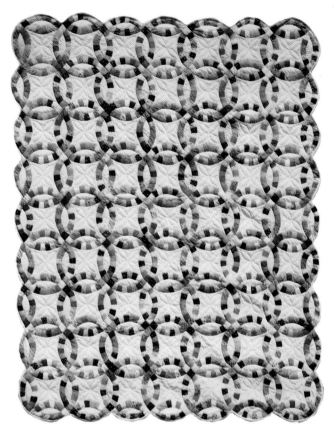

119687 - HIDDEN STAR; 92″ x 97″; cotton & polyester; made in 1987 in Missouri; hand & machine pieced, hand quilted; made of blue cotton & polyester, has the extra plump bonded polyester fill. **$403.00**

219687 - DOUBLE WEDDING RING; 84″ x 107″; made in 1987 in Missouri; machine pieced, hand quilted; made in blues, cotton/polyester fabrics, machine pieced, hand quilted, white background, has bonded polyester fill. **$345.00**

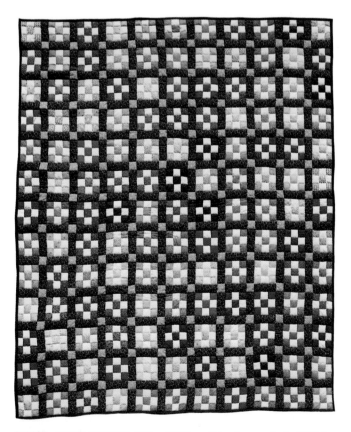

319687 - NINE PATCH; 83″ x 102″; multi-color; made in 1986 in Missouri; machine pieced, hand quilted; has the extra plump DuPont Dacron Hallofil polyester quilt batting; quilted by the piece. **$345.00**

419687 - LOG CABIN; 82″ x 105″; red; cotton/polyester; made in 1986 in Missouri; machine pieced, hand quilted; has the extra plump DuPont Dacron Hallofil polyester quilt batting. **$345.00**

120687 - FENCE RAIL; 69″ x 93″; made in Missouri; machine pieced, hand quilted; made of multi-color cotton/polyester fabric in 1985, extra plump bonded polyester fill.   **$173.00**

220687 - DRUNKARD'S PATH; 85″ x 75″; Front colors: burgundy, navy & white prints, Back colors: navy/white print; cotton/polyester, pre-washed; made in 1986 in Illinois; machine pieced, hand quilted; quilted with fine stitches around the pattern, so quilt is puffy & soft.   **$173.00**

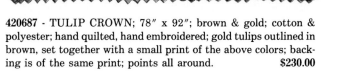

320687 - SNOWFLAKES; 83″ x 65″; white stitching on light blue fabric; pre-washed cotton/polyester; made in 1986 in Illinois; machine pieced, hand quilted; snowflakes quilted on with white thread; quilt is bordered with white piping.   **$144.00**

420687 - TULIP CROWN; 78″ x 92″; brown & gold; cotton & polyester; hand quilted, hand embroidered; gold tulips outlined in brown, set together with a small print of the above colors; backing is of the same print; points all around.   **$230.00**

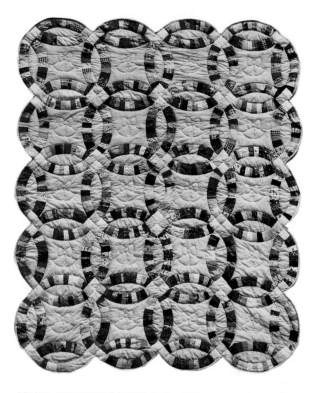

121687 - EMBROIDERED NURSERY RHYME; 77″ x 77″; cotton; red & white; hand sewn & embroidered; c. 1920 in Pennsylvania; quilted 14 st./in. in traditional feather wreaths and cross hatch. Mint condition. $403.00

221687 - WEDDING RING; 70″ x 90″; cotton-poly; made in 1986 in Missouri; machine pieced, hand quilted; variegated prints set together with light blue & white, lining is light blue. $317.00

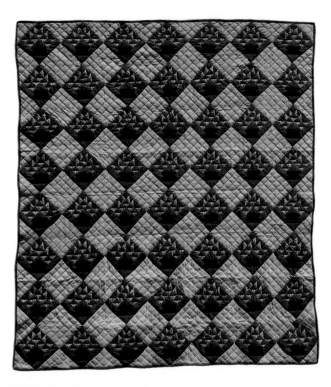

321687 - MAY BASKET; 80″ x 90″; cotton-poly; made in 1986 in Missouri; machine pieced, hand quilted; basket brown, flowers & leaves gold & green print with off-white block, off-white lining. $317.00

421687 - WINDFLOWER; 75″ x 104″; dusty rose & cream; cotton & polyester; made in 1987 in Michigan; hand tied, machine pieced; flowers have black centers; 100% extra thick bonded polyester fill; machine washable. $432.00

122687 - BIRD IN THE AIR MEDALLION; 83″ x 85″; multi-colored & pale yellow with frosted blue back; cotton & 100% polyester cotton; made in 1987 in Michigan; hand tied, machine pieced; washable & tumble dry, polyester batt & hand tied on each corner.   **$575.00**

222687 - GRANDMOTHER'S CHOICE; 74″ x 87″; slate blue, multicolored & white; 100% cotton & cotton-polyester; made in 1987 in Michigan; hand tied, machine pieced; every square was tied; washable with bonded polyester batt & a slate blue print backing; durable.   **$374.00**

322687 - LOG CABIN; 79″ x 94″; earth tones; all cotton; made in 1986 in Indiana; machine pieced, machine quilted; backing has brown print with tiny dots, batting is polyester.   **$115.00**

422687 - SUNBONNET GIRL; 72″ x 84″; different colors, borders are lime green; cotton & polyester; made in 1986 in Indiana; hand appliqued, machine quilted; backing is white muslin, polyester batting.   **$144.00**

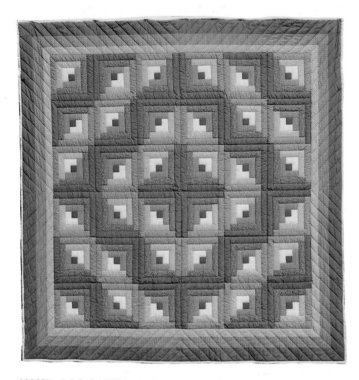

123687 - LOG CABIN; 76″ x 104″; browns & beiges; 100% cotton & poly/cotton; made in 1986 in South Carolina; machine pieced, machine quilted; polyester batting, backing is tiny tan print, fabrics are pre-washed. $345.00

223687 - LOG CABIN; 100″ x 100″; green & yellows; cotton & poly/cotton; made in 1985 in South Carolina; machine pieced, hand quilted; yellow back & binding, all fabrics were pre-washed, polyester batting. $403.00

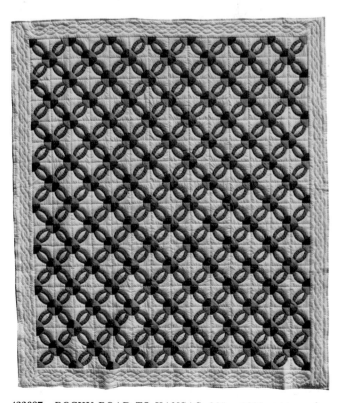

323687 - LOG CABIN; 78″ x 106″; browns & oranges; cotton & poly/cotton; made in 1986 in South Carolina; machine pieced, hand quilted; rust back, polyester batting, all fabric prewashed. $345.00

423687 - ROCKY ROAD TO KANSAS; 96″ x 109″; cotton-poly blend; made in 1987 in Missouri; hand pieced, hand quilted; made in deep rose (or mauve) & burgundy print with white fill, with bonded polyester batting. $345.00

124687 - ROYAL STAR OF MAINE; 100″ x 109″; light blue & navy print, royal blue solid & white; made in 1987 in Missouri; machine pieced, hand quilted; made in blue prints with solid blue & white, cotton-poly blend with bonded polyester batting, white lining.   **$345.00**

224687 - GARDEN WEDDING; 95″ x 106″; cotton-poly blend; made in 1986 in Missouri; machine pieced, hand quilted; multi-colored poly-cotton prints with white fill, has polyester bonded batting with white lining.   **$345.00**

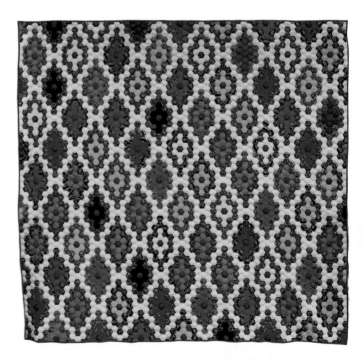

324687 - LONE STAR; 92″ x 102″; earth tones; cotton-poly blend; made in 1987 in Missouri; machine pieced, hand quilted; made of cotton polyester blends in browns & rust with small blazing stars in corners; diamond quilting in borders.   **$345.00**

424687 - GRANDMOTHER'S DIAMOND FIELD; 102″ x 108″; cotton & polyester blend; made in 1984 in Alabama; hand pieced, hand quilted; all paisley print with solid color coordinated blocks, sheet lining, quilting on each side of seam.   **$748.00**

125687 - LOG CABIN; 94″ x 97″; made in 1986 in Alabama; machine pieced, hand quilted; rose & lavender prints, rose lining, set together diagonally, all cotton, polyester batting. $460.00

225687 - TUMBLIN' STAR; 83″ x 105″; burgundy, teal & off-white; cotton; made in Alabama; machine pieced, hand quilted; all cotton top, sheet lining, rich colors. $345.00

325687 - SEVEN SISTERS; 91″ x 100″; light to dark prints; cotton & polyester; made in 1980 in Alabama; machine pieced, hand quilted. $288.00

425687 - TUMBLIN' STAR; 91″ x 94″; rust & brown; cotton; made in 1986 in Alabama; machine pieced, hand quilted; all cotton top, rust color lining, double quilting. $460.00

126687 - TRIP AROUND THE WORLD; 98" x 102"; polyester & cotton blend; made in 1980 in Tennessee; machine pieced, hand quilted. **$345.00**

226687 - GRANDMOTHER'S FAN; 72" x 92"; polyester & cotton blend; made in 1983 in Tennessee; machine pieced, hand quilted. **$345.00**

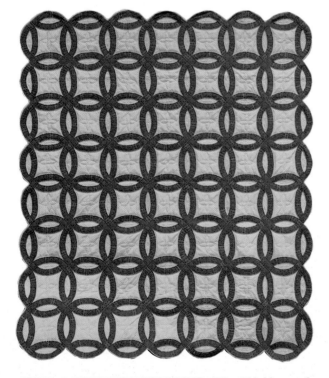

326687 - DOUBLE WEDDING RING; 85" x 98"; blues; poly-cottons; hand pieced with a little machine piecing, hand quilted. **$374.00**

426687 - DELECTABLE MOUNTAIN QUILT; 80" x 92"; slate blue; muslin; machine pieced, hand quilted; slate blue & creamy muslin; patchwork medallion center framed in a field of blue print fabric & traditional Flying Geese border. **$288.00**

101987 - HUGGABLE BEAR; 32½″ x 44″; brown & gold; cotton & cotton blends; original pattern; made 1986 in Georgia; machine pieced & hand quilted. This snuggly brown bear sits atop a gold floral print just waiting for someone to love. **$60.00**

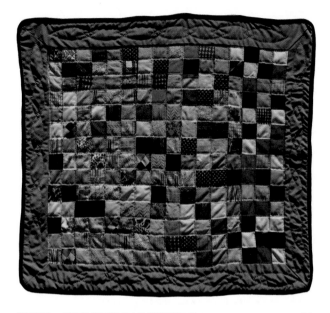

201987 - COUNTRY PATCHWORK; 45″ x 50″; green with various prints; polyester; made in 1986 in Kentucky; hand pieced, hand quilted; lining is eggshell color of brushed nylon; poly-filled; all purpose quilt; reversible; machine washable. **$70.00**

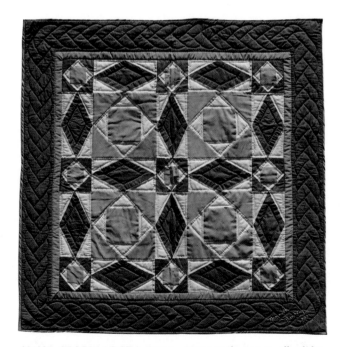

301987 - STORM AT SEA; 37½″ x 37½″; teals, aquas - all solids; poly/cottons with polyester batting; made in 1987 in Virginia & Florida; machine pieced, hand quilted; old illusionary pattern appears in motion. Continuous cable pattern in outside border. Fine quilting; pre-washed fabrics; signed & dated; double bound; mitered edges; teacher's class sample. **$98.00**

401987 - SUNRISE WALL QUILT; 27½″ x 27½″; navy, burgundy & off-white; cotton & polyester; made in 1987 in Minnesota; hand pieced, hand quilted; can be used as a table cover, bed topper or wallhanging; machine washable. **$65.00**

102987 - "TIKIS-N-KAHILIS"; 34½" x 34½"; chocolate brown on off-white; cotton-poly blends; made in 1987 in Hawaii; hand appliqued, hand quilted; a Kathleen Gerard design. Pattern depicts the idols (tikis) & torches (kahilis) used in Hawaiian ceremonies. Brown & black print outer border enhances primitive feeling of the design; ³⁄₈" quilting. **$173.00**

202987 - IRISH NINE PATCH; 35" x 35"; dark green/muslin; cotton; made in 1985 in Arkansas; machine pieced, hand quilted; nine-patch wall quilt with a lot of Irish flavor; a shamrock quilting design is used in each of the small & large muslin squares. **$70.00**

302987 - TEDDY BEAR QUILT; 43" x 43"; eggshell, yellow print, light blue & green background bordered with blocks of these colors; cotton & polyester; made in 1985-86 in Georgia; hand embroidered, hand quilted & machine pieced; batting made of cotton/polyester; hand quilted hearts. **$45.00**

402987 - LOG CABIN; 32" x 32"; cotton/polyester; made in 1986 in Illinois; machine pieced, hand quilted; wallhanging or tablecloth available in brown tones with rust, blue tones with rust or green tones with rust (pictured). **$55.00**

103987 - 4 PATCH; 36″ x 38″; pink, white & yellow; cotton & cotton/poly blend; made in 1986 in Kentucky; hand pieced, hand quilted; pastels, pink lining tie-dyed material, polyester batting, white bias binding; reversible.   **$55.00**

203987 - ALPHABET QUILT; 39½″ x 49½″; green & yellow; cotton & polyester; made in 1985 in Minnesota; hand quilted, hand appliqued; backing is green; polyester batting; machine washable; suitable for hanging.   **$167.00**

303987 - CALICO DOG; 32″ x 44″; green & yellow; cotton/cotton blends; made in 1986 in Georgia; machine pieced, hand quilted; a perky puppy in green calico & pin dot with yellow & gingham muzzle (needs a loving master); bordered in a cheerful tulip print.   **$60.00**

403987 - FARM SCENE CRIB QUILT; 42″ x 54″; blue-green multi-colored; cotton-cotton/poly; made in 1985 in Nebraska; hand quilted, machine appliqued; designed as a farm scene to hang above a crib; yarn ties in haystack represent straw; green ties in grass represent plants/grass.   **$75.00**

104987 - SMALL FLOWER; 37½″ x 46″; white background, multi-colored; cotton/polyester; made in 1986 in Georgia; machine pieced, hand quilted; different color prints for petals; hand embroidered butterflies & around petals.   **$40.00**

204987 - "LILIA HOKU"; 34″ x 34″; lavender on unbleached muslin; cotton/poly blends; made in 1987 in Hawaii; hand appliqued, hand quilted; traditional pattern celebrates the beauty of the "Star Lily." Quilting is ⅜″ apart.   **$150.00**

304987 - GRANDMOTHER'S WINDOW; 26″ x 26″; red/blue/brown; 100% cotton; made in 1986 in Arkansas; hand pieced, hand quilted; Grandmother's Cross pattern was used with white squares & set against brown to look like a decorative window in a wall.   **$70.00**

404987 - TESSELATIONS II; 27″ x 38″; hunter greens, reds, bits of yellow in prints; 100% cottons, polyester batting; made in 1986 in Virginia; machine pieced, hand quilted; finely quilted in hunter green thread; may be hung lengthwise or vertically; pattern is one block, divided & reset; signed & dated.   **$70.00**

105987 - FLOWER GARDEN; 57″ x 72″; various prints & white; cotton; made in 1950's in Kentucky; hand pieced, hand quilted; this is made of cotton scraps from the scrap bag; pink lining; white bias binding; good condition. **$145.00**

205987 - CAKESTAND; 41½″ x 56″; pink & reds; cotton & polyester; made in 1986 in Minnesota; hand pieced, hand quilted; each basket is a different red fabric; quilting is a heart & bird motif; suitable for hanging; washable. **$179.00**

305987 - CELTIC DESIGN; 29″ x 29″; red & green on white background, red binding; cotton/polyester; made in 1986 in Pennsylvania; hand quilted, hand appliqued; main design is bias tape appliqued to white background; feathered design is quilted with red thread; crosshatch quilting is done in white. **$98.00**

405987 - WHOLE CLOTH; 33″ x 43½″; bright pastels; cotton (top may have some poly); made in 1987 in Florida; hand quilted following the lines of a surreal print in bright rose, yellow, lavender & green pastel. **$190.00**

106987 - SCRAP HEARTS; 27″ x 34″; red; 100% cotton; made in 1987 in Arkansas; machine pieced, hand quilted; this heart wall quilt was made using 6 different red scraps set with muslin & then quilted using a cable design in the border. **$75.00**

206987 - "DOLPHINS & WAVES"; 27″ x 27″; unbleached muslin on blue (denim shade); cotton, poly blends; made in 1987 in Hawaii; hand appliqued, hand quilted; original pattern celebrates the playful dolphins who inhabit the island waters; background quilting is ⅜″ apart.   **$115.00**

306987 - SUNBONNET GIRL; 32½″ x 44″; pink & white; cotton & cotton blends; made in 1987 in Georgia; machine pieced, hand quilted; bearing a lace trimmed pink gingham gown with fancy apron, this miss waters a lavender calico flower.   **$60.00**

406987 - DECEMBER BLOCK; 23½″ x 23½″; cotton; made in 1986; hand pieced, hand quilted; red & green print; solid green, red & browns in center block; white background; 1st place Ohio State Fair 1986.   **$144.00**

107987 - BRIDE'S PUZZLE WALL QUILT; 32″ x 32″; rose & green; cotton & polyester; made in 1987 in Minnesota; hand pieced, hand quilted; machine washable. $81.00

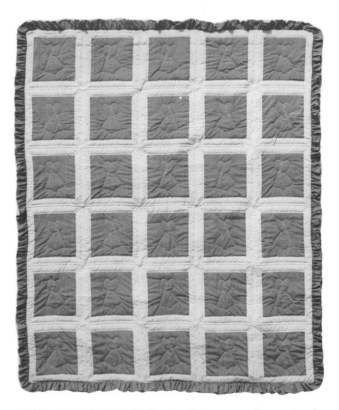

207987 - LOG CABIN; 36½″ x 43½″; cotton scraps; made in 1987 in Florida; hand quilted, machine pieced; red & white calico scraps in 7-inch blocks, blue calico centers & inner border; red calico outer border, floral back. $184.00

307987 - SUNBONNET SUE; 38″ x 55″; white background, wine, yellow & multi-print w/flowers; cotton/polyester; made in 1986 in Georgia; machine pieced, hand quilted; has a wine bonnet with embroidery floss print dress & yellow apron with white lace. $45.00

407987 - SUNBONNET SUE; 68″ x 80″; cotton polyester; made in 1987 in Mississippi; machine pieced, hand quilted, hand embroidered; pink & white quilt with Sunbonnet Sue embroidered in white on pink blocks bordered by white strips; ruffle & back are pink; polyester batting. $690.00

108987 - EIGHT POINTED STRING STAR; 82″ x 95″; multi-colors, red & black with red backing; cotton & polyester-cotton; made in 1987 in Michigan; hand tied, machine pieced; all washable with Mountain Mist batting; stars are not set in row but off-center a little. **$460.00**

208987 - WEDDING RING; 102″ x 102″; mauves (light to dark); poly-cotton; made in 1986 in Missouri; hand pieced, machine pieced, hand quilted by Amish. **$552.00**

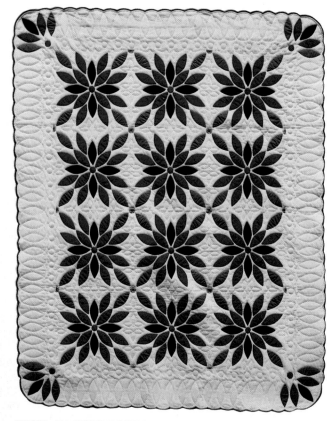

308987 - RAGGED ROBIN; 86″ x 108″; white background, red, green, black & red print; cotton; made in 1978; hand pieced, hand quilted; made by NQA winner Irene Goodrich; quilting alone took 102 hours; ribbon winning quilt. **$1,725.00**

408987 - CALICO DOG; 35″ x 45″; brown tones; cotton & cotton blends; made in 1986 in Georgia; machine pieced, hand quilted; adorable pooch created in calicos & dotted swiss arrives with his own dogbones quilted into the quilt corners. **$58.00**

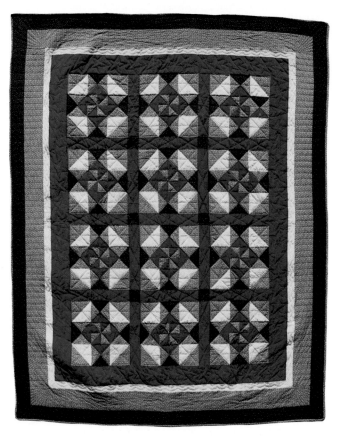

109987 - AUTUMN LEAVES; 74″ x 83″; green, tans, orange, ivory; cotton & cotton batting; made in 1930 in Pennsylvania; hand appliqued, hand embroidered, hand quilted; good condition, but pillow binding end is slightly worn. **$345.00**

209987 - "MARTHA'S STAR"; 91″ x 108″; warm brown & rust with navy & off-white; 50-50 cotton polyester blend; made in 1984; machine pieced, hand quilted; queen size; pre-shrunk; Dacron-poly batting; pillow included; signed & dated. **$478.00**

309987 - "BURGUNDIES AND BLUES"; 80″ x 91″; burgundy & blue prints, navy back; cotton/polyester, pre-washed; made in 1985 in Illinois; machine pieced, hand quilted; works well on bed or as wallhanging; durable & washable. **$345.00**

409987 - RIGHT & LEFT; 39″ x 47½″; dusty pink, forest green, light green; cotton & polyester; made in 1985 in Minnesota; hand pieced, hand quilted; quilted with hearts & tulips motif; forest green backing; machine washable. **$156.00**

110987 - BEAR'S PAW; 38″ x 38″; tones of blue & off-white with rust; cotton & polyester; made in 1986 in Illinois; machine pieced, hand quilted; wallhanging or table centerpiece. **$75.00**

210987 - WHITE ON WHITE; 82″ x 90″; white; cotton, polyester; made in 1987 in Ohio; flower design, all hand made. **$748.00**

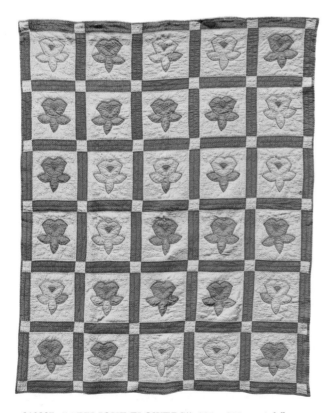

310987 - "APPLIQUE FLOWERS"; 68″ x 81″; pastel flowers set in blocks with orange; cotton; made in 1920's in Florida; machine pieced, hand quilted; 30 blocks of pastel flowers with four small hearts quilted in each corner; cheerful colors; some wear around binding & top of quilt. **$138.00**

410987 - HAWAIIAN ORCHID; 90″ x 108″; navy & orchid print applique on orchid chintz background & backing; white rose chintz & VIP cotton print applique; made in 1984 in Wisconsin; hand appliqued, hand quilted; applique is dark blue background with tiny orchid flower; placed 2nd in State Wide competition & 1st in two other quilt shows. **$1,610.00**

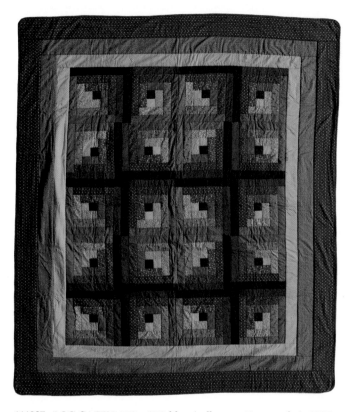

111987 - LOG CABIN; 77″ x 87″; blues/yellows; cotton; made in 1985 in Nebraska; machine pieced, machine quilted; made from a kit with Quilt As You Go method. **$202.00**

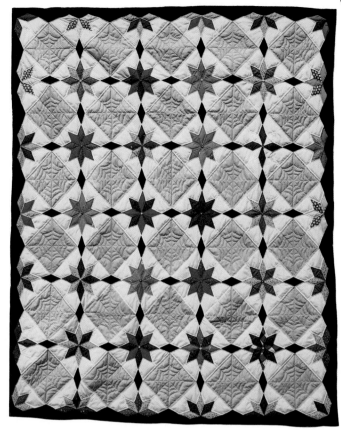

211987 - THE WANDERING DIAMOND; 82½″ x 98½″; solid black, light yellow, light purple & others; yellow, blue & wine prints; cotton/polyester; spiderweb quilting pattern inside purple blocks. **$575.00**

311987 - LONE STAR; 82½″ x 103″; background is rose, star is burgundy, rose; 100% cotton; made in 1986 in Maine; hand quilted, machine pieced; quilt is color schemed in popular shades of blue, burgundy & rose; pillow treatment is unique as a complement to the Lone Star. **$662.00**

411987 - LOG CABIN; 72″ x 90″; earth tones; 50/50 cotton & poly blends; made in 1986 in Kentucky; machine pieced, machine quilted; made of all new materials in matching colors; durable; tan lining; polyester batting. **$259.00**

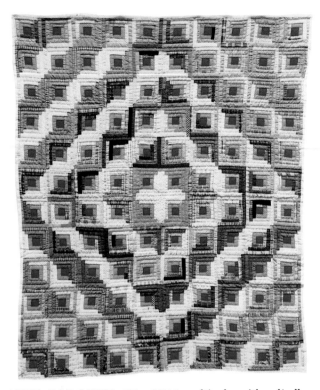

112987 - LOG CABIN; 69″ x 81½″; multi-color with red/yellow orange as focal point; cotton; made in 1955 in Kentucky; hand pieced, hand quilted; color combination is beautiful; excellent condition. **$575.00**

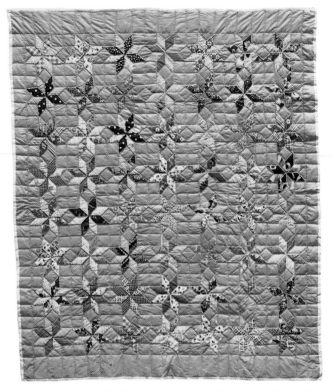

212987 - 8 POINT STAR; 72″ x 86½″; multi-color on tiny pink check; cotton; made in Kentucky; hand pieced, hand quilted; an older top that has been recently quilted; lightweight quilt. **$230.00**

312987 - TREE OF LIFE; 75″ x 86½″; predominantly blue; cotton; made in 1874 in Kentucky; hand pieced, hand quilted; blue calico with some red & burgundy, some fading, but considering the year it was made looks good; minimal damage. **$374.00**

412987 - MARTHA WASHINGTON FLOWER GARDEN; 77″ x 80″; cotton; made in 1945 in Kentucky; hand pieced, hand quilted; multi-color "flowers" on white background; quilting good. **$351.00**

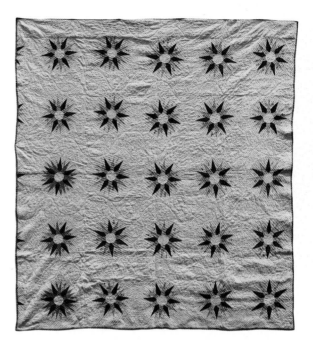

113987 - PEONY BASKET; 70″ x 73″; pink, green & tan; cotton; made in 1925 in Pennsylvania; machine pieced, hand quilted; good condition. $403.00

213987 - MARINER'S COMPASS; 75″ x 82″; navy, pink & white; cotton; made in 1888 in Pennsylvania; hand pieced, hand quilted; quilted signature reads "M.K. Smith April 26 AD 1888"; fair condition, some fabric deterioration from age. $386.00

313987 - "STEPS TO HEAVEN"; 71″ x 84″; navy & white; cotton; made in 1895 in Pennsylvania; hand pieced, hand quilted; good condition but border edges are worn. $317.00

413987 - FRIENDSHIP ALBUM; 66″ x 71″; multi-color; cotton; made in 1932 in Pennsylvania; machine pieced, hand quilted; blocks were embroidered by numerous individuals in many original patterns; excellent condition. $288.00

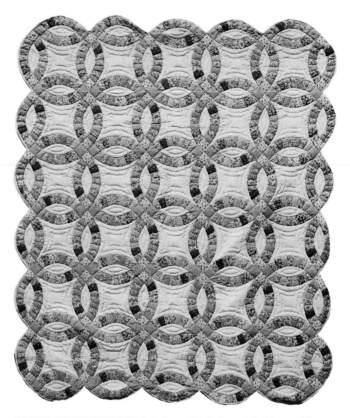

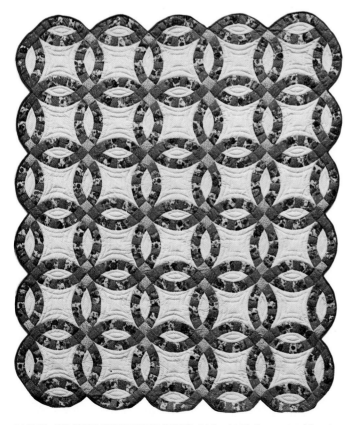

114987 - 6 POINT STAR; 64″ x 82″; red/yellow, multi-colored; cotton; made in 1955 in Kentucky; hand pieced, hand quilted; good condition. $121.00

214987 - WEDDING RING; 94″ x 112″; beige, pink, blue, gold; cotton; made in 1984 in Illinois; machine pieced, hand quilted; new condition. $270.00

314987 - BROWN WEDDING RING; 94″ x 112″; brown, gold; cotton polyester; made in 1985; machine pieced, hand quilted; new quilt. $270.00

414987 - LOG CABIN; 44″ x 44″; made in 1986 in Illinois; machine pieced, hand quilted; different shades of blue prints, rust outer border. $110.00

115987 - RED TULIP; 66″ x 79″; red, blue & green on muslin background; cotton; made in 1950 in Tennessee; hand pieced, hand quilted; excellent condition; original owner stated the quilt had been "put up & never used." $259.00

215987 - "PINEAPPLE"; 71″ x 80″; multi-colors set together with orange-yellow/red; cotton; made in 1955 in Tennessee; hand pieced, hand quilted. $374.00

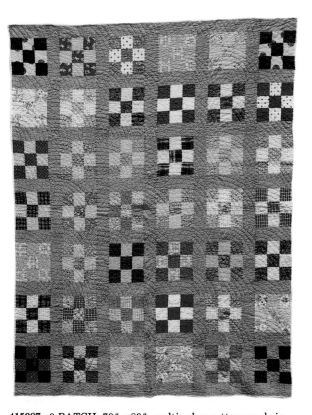

315987 - SCALLOPED FLOWER GARDEN; 62″ x 76½″; green/yellow/multi; cotton; made in 1955 in Tennessee; hand pieced, hand quilted; excellent condition. $351.00

415987 - 9 PATCH; 79″ x 80″; multi-color; cotton; made in Tennessee; hand pieced, hand quilted; light-weight quilt, set together with yellow/tan calico; very neat; not sure when made. $202.00

116987 - HEXAGON SCRAP QUILT; 73″ x 84″; pastels; cottons; made in 1930's in Iowa; hand pieced, hand quilted; over 1,800 pieces, each quilted; lightweight quilt; good condition.
$489.00

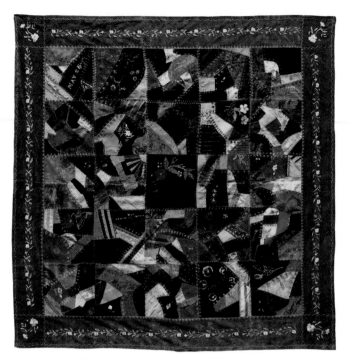

216987 - CRAZY QUILT; 73″ x 73″; made in Missouri; colorful embroidery stitching; some velvet & satin; dated July 6th, 1892; some fabrics show wear.
$850.00

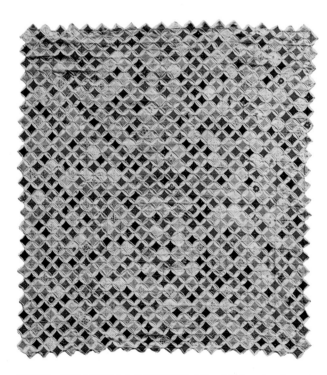

316987 - CATHEDRAL WINDOW; 86″ x 104″; polyester cotton & blends; made in 1985; hand pieced, hand quilted. **$575.00**

416987 - RED SCHOOLHOUSE CRIB QUILT; 42″ x 59″; red & white cotton & polyester; made in 1986 in Illinois; machine pieced, hand quilted; large crib quilt or wallhanging with A-B-C and 1-2-3 quilted around each schoolhouse; quilted border. **$87.00**

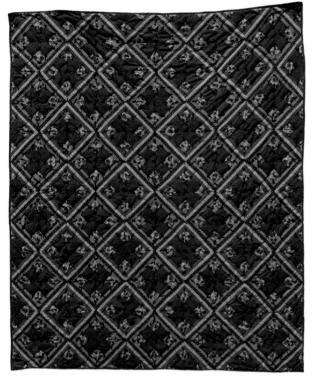

117987 - COUNTRY CLASSIC; 81″ x 96″; light brown background & backing red, gold, aqua prints; VIP cottons; made in Wisconsin; machine pieced, hand tied; has won three 1st place & three 2nd place ribbons in competitions; completed in 1982. **$403.00**

217987 - UNBLEACHED MUSLIN REVERSIBLE BLUE; 94″ x 118″; beige & blue; cotton/polyester; made in 1984 in Illinois; machine pieced, hand quilted; made from unbleached muslin & is reversible in light blue. **$230.00**

317987 - DRUNKARD'S PATH; 60″ x 87¼″; red/navy; cotton; made in 1940 in Tennessee; hand pieced, hand quilted; backing navy with pink roses; minimal damage, barely noticable. **$236.00**

417987 - GIANT DAHLIA; 80″ x 95″; rust & cream; 100% cottons, polyester ultraloft batting; made in 1985-1987 in Virginia; machine pieced, hand quilted; one-piece backing, double bound, reversible, cross-hatched background; fabrics pre-washed. **$489.00**

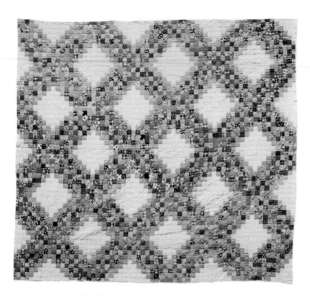

119987 - IRISH CHAIN; 77½" x 84"; multi-color with light green/white; cotton; made in 1949 in Tennessee; hand pieced, hand quilted. **$351.00**

219987 - PINK DOGWOOD; 102" x 104"; pink, white with green leaves; 60% polyester, 40% cotton; made in 1985 in Arkansas; hand pieced, hand quilted; three pillow shams included. **$460.00**

319987 - LONE STAR; 81" x 96"; brown/rust/gold prints; VIP cottons; made in 1982 in Wisconsin; hand pieced, hand quilted; 1,300 tiny diamonds were hand paper pieced quilted in feather wreaths & then background quilted in 1" graph-style; white background & backing; washable. **$863.00**

419987 - "CROSS-STITCH"; 84" x 96"; browns; cotton-polyester; made in 1985 in Illinois; machine pieced, hand quilted. **$230.00**

120987 - CRAZY QUILT; 67″ x 79″; embroidered "to pa and ma from the children"; 1890's from Missouri; various fabrics used; some show wear; some fabric dyeing & painting. $650.00

220987 - NORTH CAROLINA LILY; 90″ x 90″; red, green & white; cotton; made in 1849 in Pennsylvania; hand pieced, hand quilted; traditional pattern that is hand sewn & densely hand quilted; signed "C. Ann B. 1849"; unusual welted border; good condition, has some minor age stains & flaws. $1,150.00

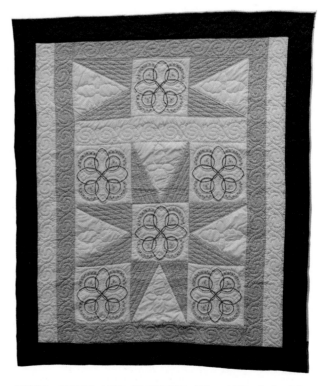

320987 - FLYING GEESE LOG CABIN; 82″ x 94½″; browns & peach; cotton; made in 1986 in Nebraska; machine pieced, machine quilted; made with Quilt As You Go technique. $259.00

420987 - RINGS AND FLOWERS; 88″ x 100″; dark pink flowers & rings of wine make the block; cotton & polyester; made in 1985 in Illinois; hand quilted; set together with small print of pink and blue flowers; points join the blocks. $219.00

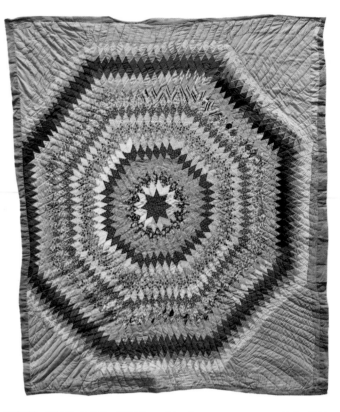

121987 - SIMPLE PLEASURES; 84″ x 99″; variety of earthtones; cotton/polyester; made in 1986 in Indiana; machine pieced, hand quilted; cream background; exhibited in 1986 AQS Show. **$363.00**

221987 - STAR; 65½″ x 77½″; multi-color star; cotton; made in 1935 in Tennessee; hand pieced, hand quilted; multi-color "stars" and blue backing; there are minor flaws typical of this age quilt. **$311.00**

421987 - STAINED GLASS; 40″ x 40″; blue & white; cotton & polyester; made in 1986 in Illinois; hand pieced, machine pieced, hand quilted; combined techniques of patchwork, padded applique & yo-yo applique; embroidery on all the seams gives it a stained glass look. **$288.00**

321987 - LOG CABIN; 96″ x 120″; brown, rose; cotton polyester; made in 1984 in Illinois; machine pieced, hand quilted; beige backing. **$230.00**

122987 - OVERALL SAM; 54″ x 88″; cotton polyester; made in 1987 in Mississippi; machine pieced, hand quilted; Overall Sam embroidered in white on denim blue set with white quilted blocks & white & blue borders; white double binding; blue back; polyester batting.   **$460.00**

222987 - PANSY; 80″ x 97″; multi-color; cotton; made in 1930 in Pennsylvania; hand appliqued, hand quilted; colorful pansies are each made in different color combinations; mint condition; one age spot.
$374.00

322987 - BROKEN STAR; 108″ x 108″; dusty blue & pink with off-white background; poly/cotton; made in 1986 in Missouri; machine pieced, hand quilted; excellent condition.   **$690.00**

422987 - BUTTERFLIES; 70″ x 70″; print & white, blue border; cotton; made in 1930's in Ohio; hand pieced, hand quilted; pieced butterflys, white background; maker unknown, quilt appears to be 1930's origin; some wear, small hole.   **$345.00**

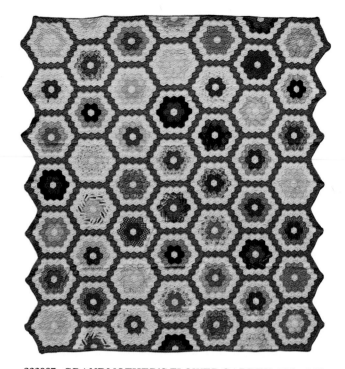

123987 - CHRISTMAS LOG CABIN; 48½″ x 48½″; reds/greens/-whites; cotton/cotton blends; made in 1987 in California; machine pieced, hand quilted; colors reflect the happy spirit of Christmas.
$202.00

223987 - GRANDMOTHER'S FLOWER GARDEN; 78″ x 86″; green; cotton; made in 1940's in Kentucky; hand pieced, hand quilted; cotton batting, lining is muslin - washed out white; good condition (binding is beginning to wear); has been in use until recently.
$144.00

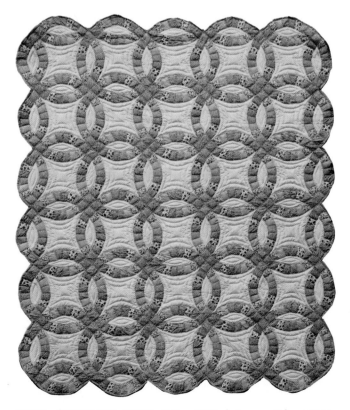

323987 - FLOWER GARDEN; 75¾″ x 84″; green/white multicolored with yellow center; cotton; made in 1955 in Tennessee; hand pieced, hand quilted; lightweight.
$202.00

423987 - WEDDING RING; 96″ x 108″; beige, pastels; cotton polyester; made in 1987 in Illinois; machine pieced, hand quilted.
$270.00

124987 - SUNFLOWER; 70″ x 86″; white background, sunflower yellow with green leaves; cotton; made in 1935 in Kansas; hand pieced, hand quilted.　　　**$1,725.00**

224987 - FOUR OF HEARTS; 26¼″ x 26¼″; Christmas reds & greens; cotton/cotton blends; made in 1987 in California; machine pieced, hand quilted; four clusters of Christmas hearts set on the diagonal; sleeve across the mid-back for insertion of a dowel to keep it hanging flat; original pattern ©1987.　　　**$81.00**

324987 - 8 POINT BROKEN STAR; 67″ x 84″; multi-color, burgundy & mixed print; cotton; made in 1950 in Tennessee; hand pieced, hand quilted; multi-print subdued in tones with a light burgundy border.　　　**$190.00**

424987 - FAN; 63¾″ x 83½″; pastels with mixed print; cotton; made in 1945 in Kentucky; hand pieced, hand quilted; an older quilt that has been exceptionally well taken care of, never used but stored away.　　　**$409.00**

125987 - "POINSETTIA" or ROSE OF SHARON; 80″ x 93″; red, white & green; cotton; made in 1930's in Kansas; hand pieced, hand quilted, hand appliqued.   **$518.00**

225987 - TRIP AROUND THE WORLD; 85″ x 108″; purple & multi-colors, all solids; poly cotton; made in Nevada in 1970's; hand pieced, hand quilted.   **$345.00**

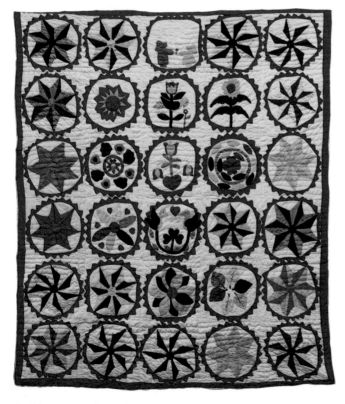

325987 - MARINER'S COMPASS; 86″ x 100″; red, white plus multi-colors; poly/cotton; made in 1970's in Nevada; hand pieced, hand quilted.   **$345.00**

425987 - STATE BIRD QUILT; 80″ x 97″; yellow & white with multi-color embroidery; made in 1970's in Nevada; hand quilted; a flower design is quilted in the yellow blocks. **$345.00**

126987 - TREE OF LIFE; 85″ x 98″; bright blue, red, orange, yellow & green; cotton & cotton-polyester blends; made in 1987 in California; hand appliqued, hand quilted; a tree with bright multi-color flowers & berries appliqued on the off-white background; similar motifs in corners; plenty of close hand quilting; red ribbon winner.   **$1,438.00**

226987 - MY HOUSE ON THE HILL; 48″ x 48″; blue/-green/red/natural calicoes; cotton/cotton blends; made in 1986 in California; machine pieced, hand quilted; this could be a child's play mat or wall decoration.   **$144.00**

326987 - DRESDEN PLATE; 71″ x 88″; pale yellow with pastel scraps; all cotton; made in 1934 in California; machine pieced, hand quilted; excellent condition, has had some use; clean.   **$345.00**

426987 - UNKNOWN; 61″ x 71″; multi-color beige print background; cotton; made in 1945 in Tennessee; hand pieced, hand quilted; quilt has multi-color stars some brown/blue/red prints/solids on small red check blocks, lightweight, minimal damage, some stains on back. **$115.00**

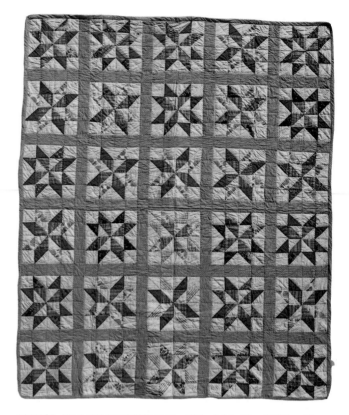

1011287 - AUTUMN LEAVES; 37″ x 37″; earth tones; cotton & cotton blends; made 1987 in California; machine pieced & hand quilted. This is reminiscent of the falling leaves of a New England autumn. $81.00

2011287 - CLAY'S CHOICE; 74″ x 88″; pink/white; 100% cotton; made in 1960 in Montana; various all-cotton fabrics on white field with pink lattices and hem binding; hand quilted & machine pieced. Never used; excellent condition. $288.00

3011287 - COWBOY KITTY; 72″ x 88″; white & blue; polyester/cotton; made in 1987 in Mississippi; machine pieced, hand quilted, hand embroidered; white squares embroidered with cowboy kitty motifs, set with blue squares quilted with star & bordered in blue & white. Blue backing matches squares. Bound in white. Polyester batting. $690.00

4011287 - ANTIQUE CARS; 78″ x 92″; denim blue & white; prewashed cotton & polyester; made in 1987 in Mississippi; machine pieced, hand quilted, hand embroidered; denim blue squares embroidered with white antique cars set together with white quilted squares & blue & white borders. Batting is polyester. The backing is white bordered with denim blue. $920.00

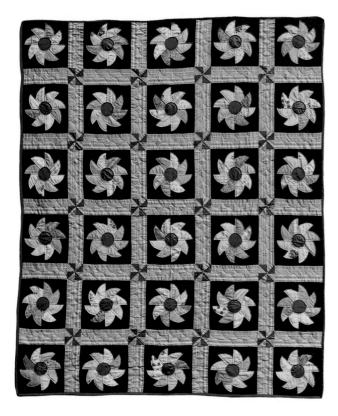

1021287 - PIN WHEEL; 93″ x 113″; print pinwheels framed in black; cotton mix, polyester batt; made in 1986 in Oregon; machine pieced, hand quilted; a few lavendar prints & lavendar striped sashing give the quilt a distinctive lavendarish look; striking when set with black. New. **$317.00**

2021287 - POSTAGE STAMP MESSAGE QUILT; 86″ x 101″; multi-color with red & blue border; cotton/cotton mix with polyester batt; made in 1985 in Oregon; machine pieced, hand quilted; contains over 4,000 1½″ squares; message is not obvious close-up but appears at a distance. New. **$460.00**

3021287 - REVERSE APPLIQUE; 77″ x 77″; all cotton (chambray), cotton batt; hand quilted, hand appliqued; rose chambray & white; cotton; original pattern made c. 1920 in Pennsylvania, hand quilted. Good condition. **$403.00**

4021287 - COURTHOUSE STEPS; 72″ x 92″; multi-pink; light to dark; silks; made in late 1920's in Illinois; hand pieced, hand quilted; anitque quilt of silks, very delicate, not for daily use. Wallhanging. New backing. **$230.00**

1031287 - WILD ROSES & BUTTERFLIES; 89″ x 94″; peach shades/brown & tan; polycotton blends; made in 1982 in Minnesota; machine pieced, hand quilted, hand appliqued; wild roses in a basket surrounded with butterflies; butterflies quilted in borders edged with scallops on 3 sides; pre-washed fabrics. **$863.00**

2031287 - LONE STAR QUILT; 100″ x 100″; sea foam green & peach; cotton & cotton/polyester; made in 1987 in Missouri; machine pieced, hand quilted. Made by Mennonite women. **$403.00**

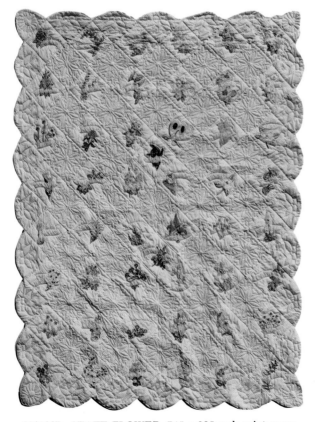

3031287 - STATE FLOWER; 74″ x 98″; pale mint green, flowers natural color; pre-washed cotton polyester; made in 1987 in Mississippi; machine pieced, hand quilted, hand embroidered; flowers for each state embroidered on white squares, set diagonally with green squares, with scalloped border. Batting is polyester & backing is same pale mint green. **$920.00**

4031287 - LOG CABIN; 48″ x 65″; pastels; polyester; made in 1987 in Illinois; machine pieced, hand quilted; new. **$58.00**

1041287 - ROSE SAMPLER; 88″ x 104″; rose, black, coordinating rose, wine prints; cottons, poly-cotton blends; made in 1983 in Minnesota; machine pieced, hand quilted; 30 blocks framed with black; signed & dated; bonded poly batting, rose & off-white print on back; pre-washed fabrics; excellent workmanship. **$805.00**

2041287 - LONE STAR QUILT; 120″ x 120″; green "mint"; cotton & polyester/cotton; made in 1987 in Missouri; machine pieced, hand quilted; made with cotton prints & polyester/cotton. Made by Mennonite women. Because of size of quilt, only 2 sides of border shown. **$460.00**

3041287 - DRESDEN PLATE; 70″ x 102″; cotton & polyester blend; made in 1987 in Mississippi; machine pieced, hand quilted, hand appliqued; Dresden Plate design in lavender, pink & blue prints on a domestic background; setting solid lavender; matching border. New. **$460.00**

4041287 - LONE STAR QUILT; 95″ x 108″; blue & rose; made in 1987 in Missouri; machine pieced, hand quilted; made with cotton prints & polyester/cotton. Made by Mennonite women. **$391.00**

1051287 - DIAMOND NINE PATCH; 75″ x 88″; aqua & yellow; cotton; made in Missouri; hand pieced, hand quilted, old top, 1920-30, hand quilted 1986 with muslin back & Dacron batting. **$196.00**

2051287 - DAHLIA; 96″ x 110″; machine pieced, hand quilted; cotton/poly fabric; forest green, off-white background & back, Dacron batting. Signed & dated. Made in Missouri in 1987. **$391.00**

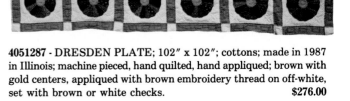

3051287 - FLY WAY; 88″ x 72″; brown; made in 1981 in New York; machine pieced, machine quilted; this quilt was made from the extra parts of men's flies from the suit factory in the quiltmaker's town. The wool pieces were the summer line in 1981. **$60.00**

4051287 - DRESDEN PLATE; 102″ x 102″; cottons; made in 1987 in Illinois; machine pieced, hand quilted, hand appliqued; brown with gold centers, appliqued with brown embroidery thread on off-white, set with brown or white checks. **$276.00**

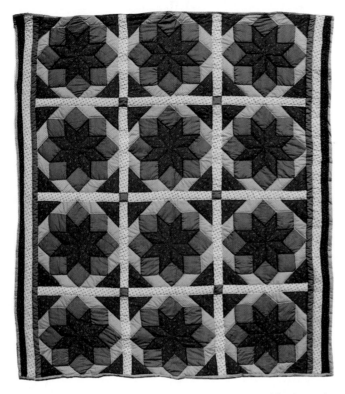

1061287 - TUMBLIN' STAR; 92″ x 102″; cotton, cotton blends; made in 1982 in Alabama; machine pieced, hand quilted; peach, burgundy print of peach/green, solid green blocks, peach lining.   **$345.00**

2061287 - JOSEPH'S QUILT; 108″ x 118″; blues, greens, yellows, pinks, purples; cotton & cotton/poly; made in 1985 in New York; machine pieced; This quilt is made with the machine flip quilting method; ''L'' shaped block.   **$288.00**

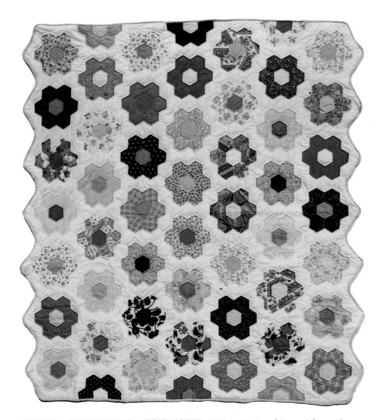

3061287 - COUNTRY PATCHWORK; 86″ x 92″; white with various prints; 50/50 poly & cotton blends; made in 1986 in Kentucky; hand pieced, hand quilted; polyester batting, white lining, scalloped sides, mint green binding; reversible, completely washable.   **$202.00**

4061287 - SPRING BOUQUET; 80″ x 100″; yellow-white; cotton/polyester; made in 1980 in Missouri; hand quilted, hand appliqued; 46 pieces hand appliqued on white to form bouquet of rose, jonquils & wind flowers. Lots of feather quilting. 1950's Mountain Mist pattern.   **$518.00**

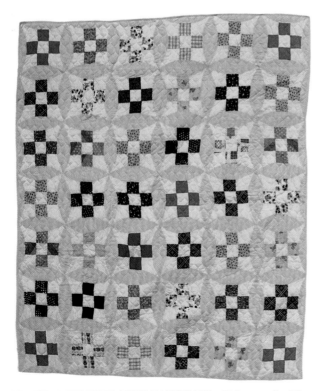

1071287 - DEVIL'S PUZZLE; 82″ x 98″; medium blue print - matching pink; cotton/polyester blend; made in 1987 in Missouri; hand pieced, hand quilted; variation of Drunkard's Path from a 1930's pattern; polyester batt, white backing.   **$460.00**

2071287 - STATE BIRDS; 67″ x 84″; coral; cotton; made in 1985; hand painted, machine quilted; bright colors, soft lining of peach, polyester padding; durable; top purchased at a sale.   **$173.00**

3071287 - IMPROVED NINE PATCH; 78″ x 92″; green & white; cotton & poly blend 50/50; made in 1986 in Kentucky; hand pieced, machine quilted; blocks are pieced of various prints set in mint green & white. Polyester padding, yellow lining.   **$173.00**

4071287 - SWEETHEART STAR; 47″ x 47″; red & white; 100% cotton; made in 1987 in Indiana; machine pieced, hand quilted; pattern from *Quilter's Newletter Magazine*, January 1987.   **$144.00**

1081287 - GIANT DAHLIA; 85″ x 97″; cotton/polyester; made in 1986 in Missouri; hand pieced, hand quilted; deep purple to lavender, peach, yellow, ivory backing, quilted feather design. New. **$518.00**

2081287 - LONE STAR; 72″ x 72″; brown, persimmon, peach, yellow, white; cotton, cotton batt; made in 1930 in Pennsylvania; hand pieced, hand quilted; maker's name on back. Good condition. **$345.00**

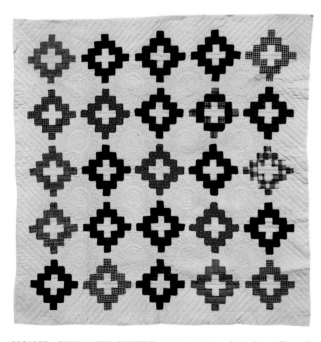

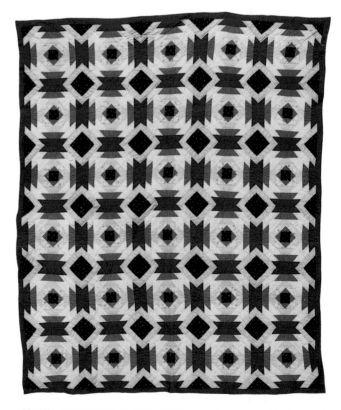

3081287 - CHIMNEY SWEEP; 67″ x 67″; multi-color calicos & white; cotton & cotton batting; made c. 1910 in Pennsylvania; machine pieced, hand quilted; mint condition. **$403.00**

4081287 - PINEAPPLE; 86″ x 102″; rose, burgundy, black accent; cotton blend, polyester batt; made in 1985 in Oregon; machine pieced, hand quilted; cheerful color scheme combined in a way that de-emphasizes the traditional pineapple pattern. **$230.00**

1091287 - SPRING FLOWER BASKETS; 86″ x 92″; bright colored baskets & flowers with white; cotton, polyester batt; made in 1986; hand pieced, hand quilted; each basket has 117 pieces. The quilt is made up of 2,365 small pieces in all. $420.00

2091287 - CHERRY BASKETS; 72″ x 72″; cream background, red & green baskets; cotton; made in 1801 in Illinois; hand pieced, hand quilted; a bride's quilt; antique red fabric used in 1987 to restore spirit of quilt; silk net finishes conservation effort. Extensive quilting, 10 stitches per inch. Documentation & extra red material will be sent to the buyer. $690.00

3091287 - LOG CABIN; 28½″ x 28½″; peach; cotton/polyester; made in 1987 in Missouri; hand quilted; bonded polyester batt; wallhanging or doll quilt. $45.00

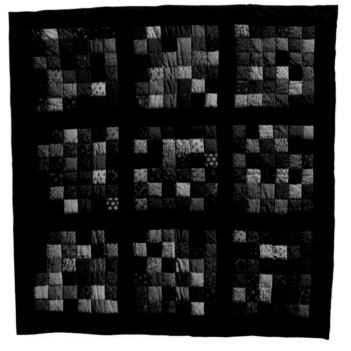

4091287 - PATCHWORK; 42″ x 42″; navy blue; cotton/polyester; made in 1987 in Missouri; machine pieced, hand quilted; extra plump bonded polyester fill. $55.00

1101287 - BOUGAINVILLEA; 26½″ x 26½″; red on unbleached muslin; poly-cotton blends; made in 1987 in Hawaii; hand appliqued, hand quilted; design by Elizabeth Root. A popular ornamental, the bougainvillea is found in many colors & varieties in Hawaii, where it blooms almost continuously. Quilting ⅜″ apart.　**$115.00**

2101287 - HAWAIIAN BABY ROSE; 27½″ x 27½″; dusty rose on white; poly-cotton blends; made in 1987 in Hawaii; hand appliqued, hand quilted; a Kathy Gerard pattern. This pattern, also called "Lokelani," represents the floral symbol for the island of Maui.　**$133.00**

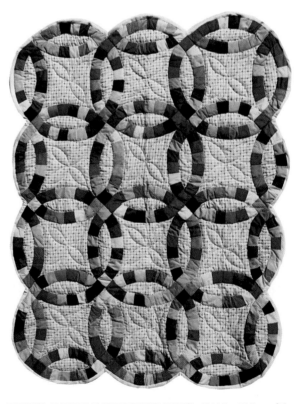

3101287 - ROSE OF SHARON; 39″ x 39″; dusty blue/dusty pink; cotton poly; made in 1986 in Missouri; machine pieced, hand quilted; cotton/poly fabric, dusty blue/dusty pink, off-white background & back. Needle punch flowers (wears & washes well). Signed & dated.　**$127.00**

4101287 - DOUBLE WEDDING RING; 40½″ x 51″; multi-colored solids with print fill; cotton/polyester; made in 1987 in Missouri; machine pieced, hand quilted; extra plump polyester fill.　**$60.00**

1111287 - LOG CABIN; 48″ x 48″; navy blue; cotton/polyester; made in 1987; machine pieced, hand quilted; extra plump bonded polyester fill. $55.00

2111287 - STAR; 36″ x 36″; pinks & blues; cotton & polyester blends; made in 1985 in Pennsylvania; machine pieced, hand quilted; washable, polyester batting. $58.00

3111287 - DOUBLE WEDDING RING; 41″ x 41″; pastel prints & unbleached muslin; cotton muslin, polyester-cotton blends; made in 1987 in Pennsylvania; machine pieced, hand quilted; washable - all new pre-washed materials; polyester batting. $115.00

4111287 - FLOWER BASKET WALLHANGING; 35″ x 41″; assorted on off-white; brown edge; cottons & polyester blends; made in 1985 in Pennsylvania; hand pieced, hand quilted; unusual texture surface, hanging is reversible if preferred; made of folded hexagons; polyester batting. $115.00

1121287 - AMISH FANS: 42″ x 42″; black with various solid colors; 100% cotton; made in 1987 in Minnesota; machine pieced, hand quilted; quilted with black thread on black & in the ditch around & on fans. Pre-washed fabrics; chalk used to mark quilting. **$144.00**

2121287 - PINWHEELS; 45″ x 53½″; white/pastels; various cotton scraps, gingham border; made in 1987 in Michigan; machine pieced, hand quilted; 100% polyester batting, baby quilt; pastel pinwheels, white muslin bottom. **$110.00**

3121287 - SEMINOLE SUNSET; 25″ x 45″; assorted prints & solid colors; cotton & polyester blend; made in 1987 in Mississippi; machine pieced, hand quilted; a seminole patchwork design wallhanging in bright prints & solid colors; dark gold backing. **$115.00**

4121287 - LOG CABIN; 28½″ x 28½″; maroon; cotton/polyester; made in 1987 in Missouri; hand quilted; wallhanging or a doll quilt, bonded polyester batt. **$45.00**

1131287 - HEARTS AND FLOWERS; 42½″ x 42½″; true red on white, red binding; red cotton, white poly-cotton; made in 1987 in Illinois; hand quilted, hand appliqued; single piece red Hawaiian design appliqued on white background with Hawaiian style quilting closely outlining the design & filling spaces. $345.00

2131287 - LOG CABIN; 43″ x 56″; pastels; polyester; made in 1987 in Illinois; machine pieced, hand quilted; traditional pattern, soft pastels. New. $58.00

3131287 - GRANNIE'S HOUSE; 39″ x 41½″; bright primary colors; calico, polyester & cotton blends, 100% cottons; made in Michigan; machine pieced, hand quilted; 100% polyester batting. Backing is pastel striped fabrics. $60.00

4131287 - RAINBOWTIES; 28″ x 36″; variegated solids/black; 100% cotton; made in 1987 in Wisconsin; machine pieced, hand quilted, hand pieced; rainbow solids & black were hand pieced into squares & then machine pieced & hand quilted. $144.00

1141287 - SKY PILOT; 46″ x 56″; navy/burgundy border - blues, greens; cotton - cotton/poly blend; made in 1986 in Wisconsin; machine pieced, hand quilted; SKY PILOT is another name for a preacher. A familiar song from the 1960's by that name the quiltmaker heard on the radio & it stuck.   **$340.00**

2141287 - FOREVERGREEN; 31″ x 38″; earth tones, rust border; cotton/cotton poly blend; made in 1985 in Wisconsin; machine pieced, hand quilted; wallhanging depicts a house and evergreen tree reflecting itself in water & sees itself forever young, forever green.   **$230.00**

3141287 - FLIGHT OVER THE PINES; 50″ x 58″; original pattern used with permission from *Color for Quilters* by Susan McKelvey; rust/greens; cotton, cotton/poly blends; made in 1985 in Wisconsin; machine pieced, hand quilted; geese-chase around the border & repeated throughout the quilt in the trees & quilting. Houses & trees sit on the hill.   **$340.00**

4141287 - 8 POINT STAR; 85½″ x 77″; multi-print; cotton; made in 1945 in Tennessee; hand pieced, hand quilted; interlocked by blue calico squares.   **$202.00**

1151287 - COLONIAL LADY; 72″ x 73″; multi-color on beige; cotton; made in 1985 in Tennessee; hand pieced, hand quilted; nice quilt with multi-color "ladies" on beige background; has a red border. **$144.00**

2151287 - VIRGINIA REEL TYPE; 75½″ x 94″; blue/white/burgundy; cotton; made in 1986 in Tennessee; hand pieced, hand quilted. **$328.00**

3151287 - SEVEN SISTERS; 81″ x 93″; red, blue, light green; cotton; made in 1984 in Kentucky; machine pieced, hand quilted. **$345.00**

4151287 - GARLAND OF ROSES; 80″ x 96″; pink & green; cotton; made in 1985 in Kentucky; hand pieced, hand quilted, hand appliqued; feather pattern quilting. **$345.00**

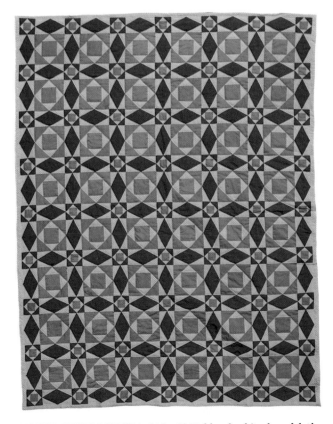

1161287 - STAR OF BETHLEHEM; 78″ x 78″; red/blue/pink calico; cotton; made in 1935 in Kentucky; hand pieced, hand quilted; this is unique kind of quilt, made in old-fashioned coordinated colors of calico. **$351.00**

2161287 - BOUQUETS OF ROSES; 82″ x 97″; pink, green & yellow; cotton; made in 1985 in Kentucky; hand quilted, hand appliqued; quilt is pictured in *Family Circle Decorating*, March 1986. **$345.00**

3161287 - STORM AT SEA; 81″ x 104″; blue & white; broadcloth; made in 1985 in Illinois; hand pieced, hand quilted; made entirely by hand, two shades of blue. New. **$403.00**

4161287 - EIGHT POINTED STAR; 87″ x 103″; shaded browns, golds, print calico; cotton/polyester; made in 1985 in Illinois; hand pieced, hand quilted; shaded browns & dark brown cross-stitch; set together with print calico of brown leaves & gold flowers. **$213.00**

1171287 - LOG CABIN; 84″ x 96″; chocolate browns; cotton/polyester top/100% ecru cotton backing; made in 1985 in Tennessee; machine pieced, hand quilted; beautiful rich browns; approximately 7 stitches per inch.   **$432.00**

2171287 - MONKEY WRENCH; 88″ x 103″; pink & rose tones; cotton/polyester blend fabric; made in 1987 in Alabama; machine pieced, hand quilted; thick quilt; makes a lovely comforter for a queen size bed.   **$458.00**

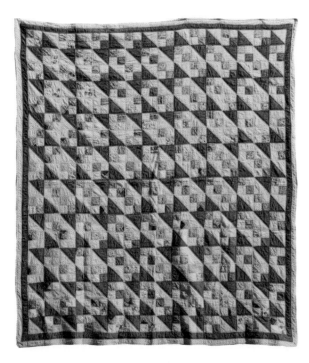

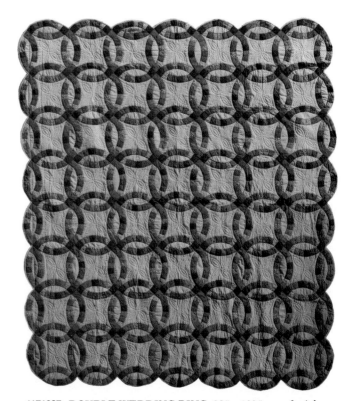

3171287 - JACOB'S LADDER; 78″ x 85″; cotton print & domestic cotton batting; made in 1931; domestic lining hand made.   **$259.00**

4171287 - DOUBLE WEDDING RING; 88″ x 103″; rose & pink tones; cotton/polyester blend fabric; made in 1984 in Alabama; machine pieced, hand quilted; most popular pattern, flower quilting between each ring.   **$458.00**

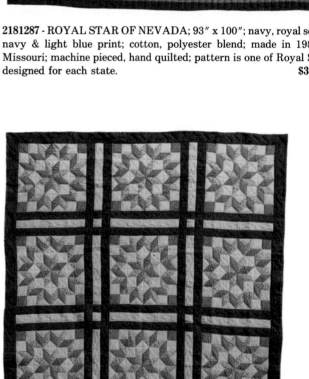

1181287 - DOUBLE WEDDING RING; 94″ x 94″; medium blue with royal blue, pink & white; cotton; made in 1987 in Illinois; machine pieced, hand quilted. **$253.00**

2181287 - ROYAL STAR OF NEVADA; 93″ x 100″; navy, royal solids, navy & light blue print; cotton, polyester blend; made in 1987 in Missouri; machine pieced, hand quilted; pattern is one of Royal Stars designed for each state. **$345.00**

3181287 - ROYAL STAR OF MICHIGAN; 93″ x 100″; navy, royal, light blues & white; cotton-polyester blend; made in 1987 in Missouri; machine pieced, hand quilted; one of 50 Royal Stars designed by a lady for *Quilt World Magazine*. **$345.00**

4181287 - CARPENTER'S WHEEL or ECCENTRIC STAR; 82″ x 108″; made in 1987; hand pieced, hand quilted; all new percale & muslin material, polyester batting, muslin lining. **$345.00**

1191287 - FLYING SWALLOWS; 89″ x 99″; dark blues, royals & light blue; cotton-polyester blend; made in 1987 in Missouri; machine pieced, hand quilted; larger variation of the traditional Flying Swallows blocks, done in 3 shades of blue & with white fill. Quilting is done in triangles. **$345.00**

2191287 - "MAKO'A" - Coral Head of the Sea; 44″ x 46″; ocean blue applique & border on white background; applique & background is polyester/cotton blended Imperial Broadcloth, quilt backing is blue calico; made in 1987 in Marshall Islands; hand pieced, hand quilted, hand appliqued; design depicts the coral heads of the sea & the moving ocean currents; done in traditional Hawaiian quilting manner; machine wash & dry. **$455.00**

3191287 - "KE KALAUNA ME KA LEI" - Crown and Wreath; 41½″ x 72″; rust applique & border/bronco background; applique & background is Imperial Broadcloth polyester/cotton; quilt backing is 100% cotton VIP calico; made in 1986 in Marshall Islands; hand pieced, hand appliqued, hand quilted; Royal Hawaiian Crown given a cameo effect; wallhanging or lap quilt; machine wash & dry. **$564.00**

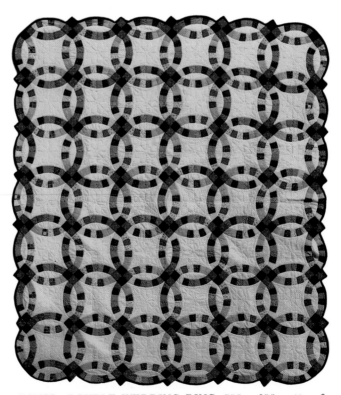

4191287 - DOUBLE WEDDING RING; 75″ x 85″; cotton & polyester; made in 1987 in Georgia; machine pieced, hand quilted; all color fabrics on white background of cotton & polyester. **$230.00**

1201287 - LOVE RING; 98″ x 106″; shades of blue; cotton; made in 1987 in Illinois; machine pieced, hand quilted; new. $265.00

2201287 - ROYAL STAR OF RHODE ISLAND; 90″ x 93″; pink, maroon & pink, maroon print; percale; made in Ohio; hand pieced, hand quilted; polyester batting. $345.00

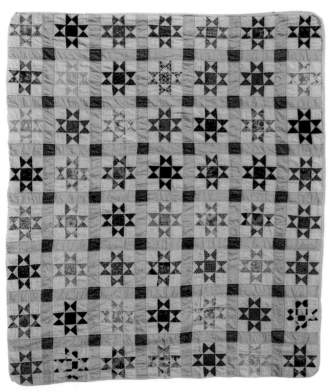

3201287 - OHIO STAR; 78″ x 86″; scrap with pink & white settings, cream colored back & binding; cotton & blends; made in 1962 in Arkansas; hand pieced, hand quilted; scraps in this never used quilt sparkle. Cotton batt. $288.00

4201287 - BABY BLOCKS; 72″ x 93″; chocolate brown print, luggage tan, rose print; broadcloth combined with prints; made in 1985 in Illinois; machine pieced, hand quilted; new. $374.00

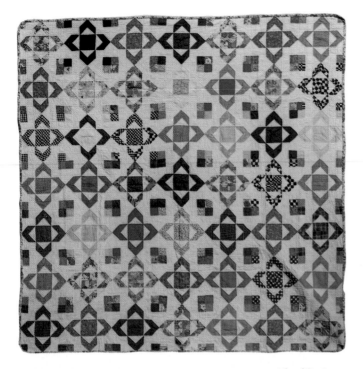

1211287 - PUSS IN THE CORNER; 86″ x 86″; scrap with white top, medium blue backing, print binding; cotton & blends; made in 1962 in Arkansas; hand pieced, hand quilted; old-fashioned looking quilt made with cotton batt. Never used. **$288.00**

2211287 - DRESDEN PLATE; 91″ x 92″; navy polka dot, navy print, light blue print, light blue solid; cotton & polyester; made in 1987 in Arkansas; machine pieced & appliqued, hand quilted. **$328.00**

3211287 - 8 POINT STAR; 73″ x 88″; predominantly red & white; polyester & cotton; made in 1969; hand pieced, hand quilted; most of the blocks are made of cotton flowered print, a few are solid. **$190.00**

4211287 - CENTENNIAL LILY; 104″ x 104″; orange & yellow lily with green stems & leaves on white background & white backing - orange binding; cotton blends; made in 1970 in California; machine pieced, hand appliqued, hand quilted; very fine applique work done on lilies, excellent quilting all over, feather circles quilted in large squares, won many blue ribbons. Dacron batt. **$690.00**

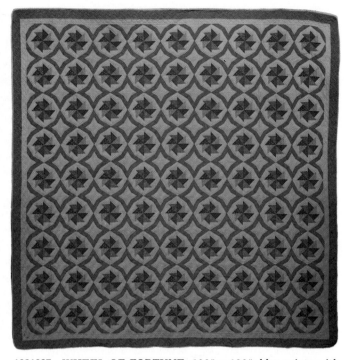

1221287 - WHEEL OF FORTUNE; 106″ x 106″; blue prints with unbleached muslin; cotton prints & unbleached muslin; made in 1986 in Illinois; machine pieced, hand quilted; made from 9 different prints combined with the soft color of muslin & is large enough to touch the floor on a king size bed. New. **$460.00**

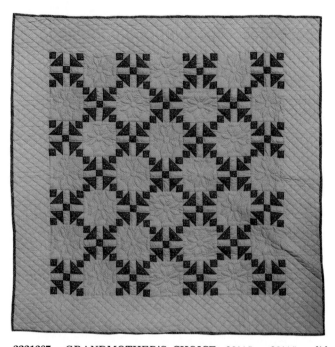

2221287 - GRANDMOTHER'S CHOICE; 83½″ x 83½″; solid lavender & burgundy print; 100% cotton & cotton/polyester blend; made in 1987 in Minnesota; machine pieced, hand quilted; flowers quilted on plain blocks, shadow quilting on patchwork blocks. All pre-washed fabrics. Backing is burgundy print to match top. Polyester batting. Clean & new. **$690.00**

3221287 - PINEAPPLE; 23″ x 41″; gray mini dot on white background; cotton, percale; made in 1987 in Hawaii; hand appliqued, hand quilted; designed by Darlene Tom. Clam shell quilting on design; background quilting ³⁄₈″ apart. **$184.00**

4221287 - FLOWER GARDEN; 82″ x 62¾″; light yellow & mixed prints; cotton; made in 1935 in Kentucky; hand pieced, hand quilted; lightweight quilt; good stitching, the colors blend well (made during Depression era). **$202.00**

1231287 - FLOWER GARDEN; 55″ x 81″; multi-color fabric flowers & border on eggshell background; cotton & polyester; made in 1987 in Georgia; machine embroidered, hand quilted. **$75.00**

2231287 - VAR. PINEAPPLE; 81″ x 98″; old rose; cotton; made in 1982 in California; hand pieced, hand quilted; old rose, light & dark reverse print. Dye-set & pre-shrunk, Amish quilting. **$403.00**

3231287 - CHURN DASH; 70″ x 86½″; pink/blue/white; cotton; made in 1874 in Kentucky; hand pieced, hand quilted; lightweight quilt with old-fashioned prints with blocks of blue made 113 years ago. **$179.00**

4231287 - POSTAGE STAMP; 65″ x 79″; red/navy/mixed prints & solids; cotton; made in 1935 in Tennessee; hand pieced, hand quilted; very colorful quilt. **$524.00**

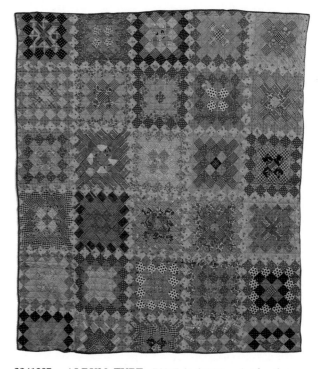

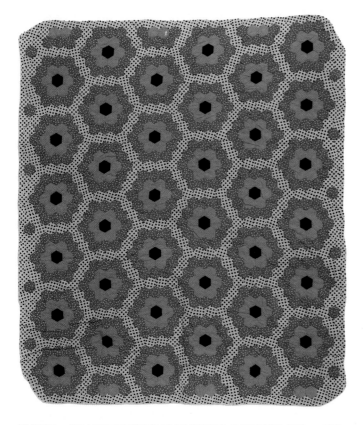

1241287 - STORMY SEAS; 80″ x 98″; medium country blue & white; cotton; made in 1980 in California; hand pieced, hand quilted; all materials have been pre-shrunk & dye-set, combines two traditional patterns using light & reverse prints. Amish quilting. **$403.00**

2241287 - ALBUM TYPE; 76½″ x 84½″; mixed colors, bluish/grey backing, red binding; cotton; made in 1950 in Kentucky; hand pieced, hand quilted; quilt looks very country. Excellent condition. **$288.00**

3241287 - GRANDMOTHER'S FLOWER GARDEN; 72″ x 85″; orange solid & print, black polka dot & white; cotton; made in 1979 in Alabama; hand pieced, hand quilted. **$219.00**

4241287 - NORTH CAROLINA STAR, a Variation; 56½″ x 72″; red, navy, camel, blue; 100% cotton, 100% poly batting; made in 1986 in Wisconsin; machine pieced, hand quilted; cheerful red throw, tiny stitches form a unique circular quilting pattern. Designed & made by a prize winning Wisconsin quilter. New. **$460.00**

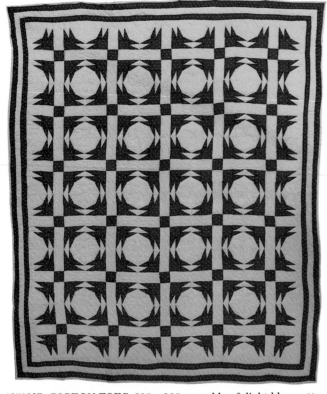

1251287 - PIGEON TOES; 83″ x 96″; navy blue & light blue; cotton & polyester blends, polyester batting; made in 1986 in Pennsylvania; machine pieced, hand quilted; completely washable, tiny white bows in navy print, quilted bows in plain areas. $403.00

2251287 - TRIP AROUND THE WORLD; 77″ x 92″; multi-colored; cotton, cotton blends; made in 1986 in Alabama; hand pieced, hand quilted; two poly batting inside, sheet lining. $288.00

3251287 - LOG CABIN; 86″ x 110″; blue; cotton/polyester; made in 1987 in Missouri; machine pieced, hand quilted; plump bonded polyester fill. $345.00

4251287 - DREAM CHAIN; 80″ x 98″; lavender; cotton; made in 1972 in California; hand pieced, hand quilted; old pattern using many purple scraps, all new material. Amish quilters. $345.00

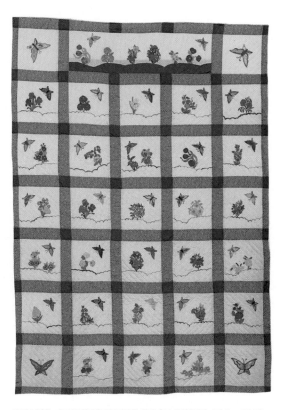

1261287 - BIRDS OF A FEATHER; 80″ x 107″; shades of tans, greens & yellows; cotton & cotton blends, unbleached domestic background; made in 1987 in Kentucky; hand quilted, hand appliqued. $345.00

2261287 - BUTTERFLIES IN GARDEN; 72″ x 100″; multi-color flowers & butterflies on white background with dark green & green floral border; cotton & polyester; made in 1987 in Kentucky; machine pieced, hand quilted; tube painted flowers & butterflies, multi-colors on white background, dark solid green & green floral paint border. $202.00

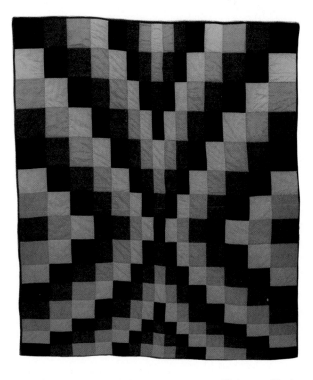

3261287 - BIRD-IN-HAND; 90″ x 104″; blues & whites; cotton with polyester batting; made in 1986 in Oregon; machine pieced, hand quilted; has a lovely geometric design. Excellent. $288.00

4261287 - MAYAN TEMPLE; 96″ x 106″; gold, brown, black & white; cotton with polyester batting; made in 1986 in Oregon; machine pieced, hand quilted; has striking yet simple design. $173.00

101388 - DRESDEN PLATE; 73½″ x 84″; blue & white; all cotton; made c. 1940 in Michigan; machine pieced, hand appliqued, hand quilted. Plain blue & blue print on white cotton; white backing. **$690.00**

201388 - FANS FOR MY LADY; 85″ x 100″; 100% cotton; made in 1987 in Wisconsin; machine pieced, hand quilted; a soft looking quilt made with blue, rose, lavender and off-white; lots of fans & quilted flowers. **$389.00**

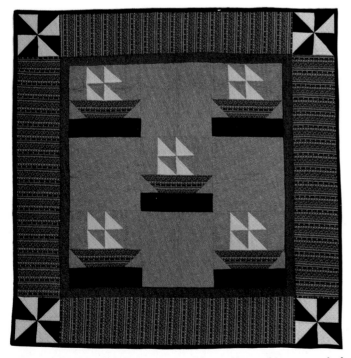

301388 - SHIP OF DREAMS; 36″ x 36″; blue, red/rose, white; pre-washed 100% cotton (polyester lowloft batting); made in 1987 in North Carolina; machine pieced, hand quilted; lots of hand quilting in clamshells, cables & laurel wreaths; prepared for hanging; perfect for child's room or beach house. **$156.00**

401388 - DUTCH BIRDS; 88″ x 108″; parchment or off-white; polyester & cotton; made in 1987 in Pennsylvania; machine pieced, hand quilted; plain top, polyester fill; a lot of fine quilting. **$662.00**

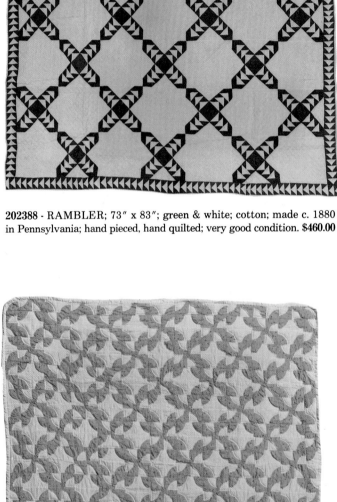

102388 - BLUE STAR; 78″ x 89″; blue & white; cotton; made in 1977 in Kentucky; hand pieced, hand quilted. **$288.00**

202388 - RAMBLER; 73″ x 83″; green & white; cotton; made c. 1880 in Pennsylvania; hand pieced, hand quilted; very good condition. **$460.00**

302388 - LONE STAR; 102″ x 105″; brown & rust; cotton/polyester blend; made in 1987 in Missouri; machine pieced, hand quilted; brown & rust with variegated prints with cream background; diamond zig-zag border with small blazing star in corners; Dupont Dacron polyester batting. **$345.00**

402388 - DRUNKARD'S PATH; 92″ x 92″; peach print & white with plain peach backing; cotton blend; made in 1986 in Arkansas; hand pieced, hand quilted; soft color. **$230.00**

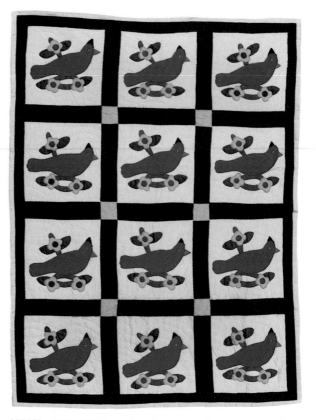

103388 - FLOWER GARDEN; 90″ x 104″; multi-colored with off-white background; cotton & polyester; made in 1979 in Tennessee; machine pieced, hand quilted; flower garden is set together with beige & blue pin dots. **$460.00**

203388 - RED BIRD; 72″ x 90″; red, yellow, brown & black; cotton blends; made in 1987 in Kentucky; hand pieced, hand quilted; hand appliqued; white lining; polyester batting. **$173.00**

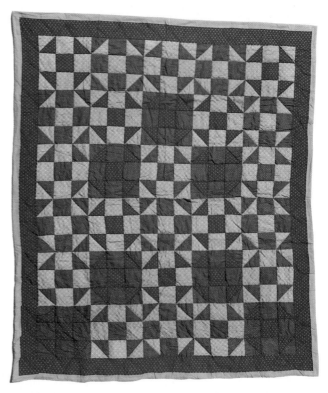

303388 - UNKNOWN; 77″ x 90″; browns, yellows, greens & oranges; cotton-cotton/polyester; made in 1984 in Ohio; machine pieced, hand quilted. **$748.00**

403388 - SHOO FLY; 71″ x 84″; red, light blue, dark blue; cotton calicos/polyester batting/muslin back; made in 1986 in New York; machine pieced, hand quilted; reproduction of older pattern with alternating blue & red blocks. **$460.00**

104388 - ROLLING STONE; 86″ x 86″; pink, yellow & green; old cotton fabric; made in late 1800's in Pennsylvania; hand pieced, hand quilted; 25 (11″) blocks of Rolling Stone with sawtooth border & quilted cable pink edge; 2 small repairs on front with old material. $345.00

204388 - PATCHWORK; 78″ x 87″; multi-colored; silk & rayon; made in 1930's in Washington; machine pieced; old silk & rayon quilt with loop border (needs some repair). $144.00

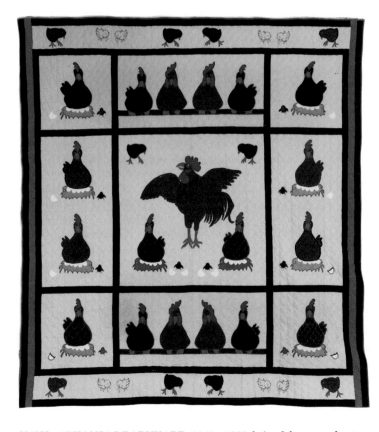

304388 - ARKANSAS BARNYARD; 104″ x 108″; beige & brown; polyester & cotton blend; made in 1987 in Arkansas; hand pieced, hand appliqued, hand quilted; poly batting. $575.00

404388 - STACKED BRICKS; 81″ x 103″; Assrtd., border fine floral & fruit print, back - forest green, sashing - forest green print; made in 1987 in Indiana; machine pieced, hand quilted; chain quilted stacked bricks with elegant tassel quilted border; fabric pre-washed; bonded poly-batting. $575.00

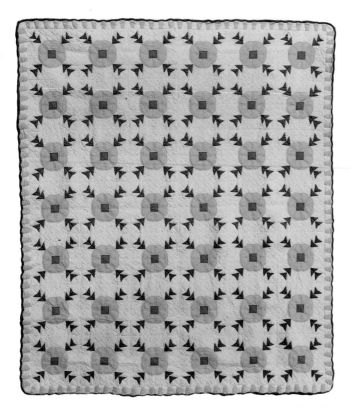

105388 - PIECED ROSE; 80″ x 94″; pink & green with white background; broadcloth, sheet for lining, polyester filling; made in 1987 in Florida; hand pieced, hand quilted; 1930's design, also called AMISH BLUME. **$345.00**

205388 - NINE PATCH; 66″ x 78″; red & white with gray polka dots; cotton; made c. 1920 in Virginia; hand quilted; 9 patch mixed with plain red; antique look. **$345.00**

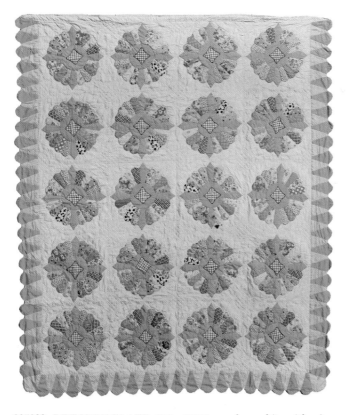

305388 - DRESDEN PLATE; 79″ x 91½″; peach on white with misc. scraps; cottons & blends with sheet backing, cotton batting; machine pieced, hand quilted; dominate peach on white background; top was machine pieced around 1930 with hand quilting & completed in 1986 in Wisconsin. **$345.00**

405388 - TEDDY BEAR; 44″ x 50″; red, red pindot, yellow check & beige; cotton & cotton blends; made in 1987 in Wisconsin; hand embroidered, machine pieced, machine quilted; eggshell lining, polyester batting; lots of teddy bears sitting in a row. **$60.00**

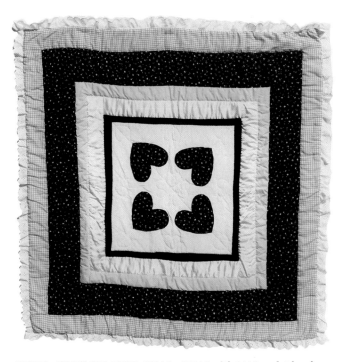

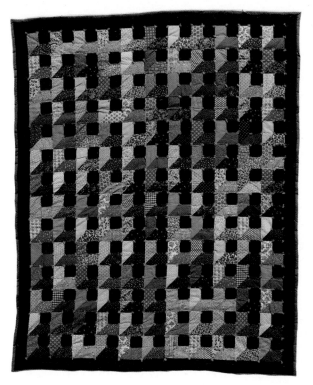

106388 - FOUR HEARTS; 39½″ x 39½″ with 1½″ eyelet border; black, white, aqua & white satin & muslin; satin, gingham, muslin, calico with 100% polyester batting; made in 1987 in Michigan; machine pieced, hand quilted; reversible gingham bottom; eyelet trim on edge. $60.00

206388 - ATTIC WINDOWS; 75″ x 92″; "antique" colors with black & gray; cotton & polyester; made in 1987 in Michigan; hand tied, machine pieced; all washable fabric with a polyester batting. $230.00

306388 - VARIATION CONTINUOUS RIBBON "CHRISTMAS IN JULY"; 41″ x 41″; red, blue, green, gold; cottons, polyblends, sateen; made in 1984 in California; hand pieced, hand quilted in the ditch; combining contemporary floral prints with solid intense colors gives the feel of the explosion of the winter terraces of color in So. California; border is Pakistani strip work. $432.00

406388 - AUNT CLARA'S STAR; 83″ x 94″; blue; cotton & cotton blends; made in 1986 in Arkansas; hand pieced, hand quilted; assorted colored stars set together with blue. $230.00

107388 - SUNFLOWER APPLIQUE; 78″ x 94″; solids of dark yellow, green & brown on white; cotton; made c. 1945 in Ohio; machine pieced, hand quilted, hand appliqued; triple bordered; nice diagonal & outline quilting plus an oblong abstract sunflower quilted in center; maker unknown. $489.00

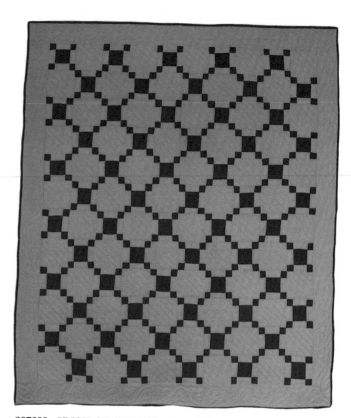

207388 - IRISH CHAIN; 92″ x 108″; blue light/dark; polyesters - cottons; made in 1987 in Illinois; machine pieced, hand quilted. $230.00

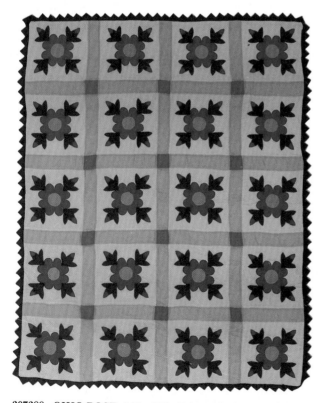

307388 - OHIO ROSE; 64″ x 80″; pink, green & white; percale; made in 1980 in Kentucky; hand quilted, machine appliqued. $230.00

407388 - SAMPLER QUILT OF 24 PATTERNS; 78″ x 101″; red, navy, light blue; 100% cotton; made in 1985 in Missouri; hand pieced, hand quilted; sampler quilt with 24 hand pieced & quilted traditional blocks; good condition, one small sun bleached area. $460.00

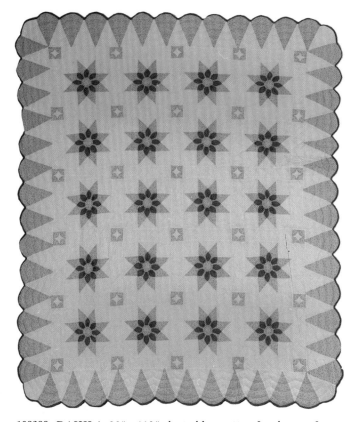

108388 - DAHILA; 96″ x 110″; dusty blue; cotton & polyester & cotton; made in 1987 in Missouri; machine pieced, hand quilted; made with cotton prints & polyester & cotton; made by Mennonite women in Missouri. $403.00

208388 - SPIDER WEBB; 82″ x 99″; all colors of print with solid; cotton with some polyester; made in 1979; machine pieced, hand quilted; this is one of Maggie Malone's patterns, quilted by the piece. $213.00

308388 - FLEUR DE LIS; 36″ x 36″; gray, blue & printed band of pre-washed cotton; made in 1986 in West Virginia; machine pieced, hand quilted, hand appliqued; inspired by Old English tills; signed & dated; a sleeve on back for hanging. $172.50

408388 - LOG CABIN; 82″ x 102″; shades of blue; cotton; made in 1987 in Kentucky; machine pieced, hand quilted; quilting follows outline of logs. $345.00

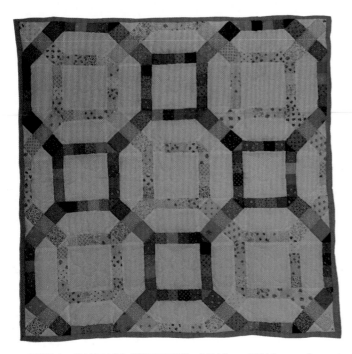

109388 - GARDEN WEDDING; 39½″ x 39½″; purple; cotton/polyester; made in 1987 in Missouri; machine pieced, hand quilted; extra plump bonded polyester fill.   **$60.00**

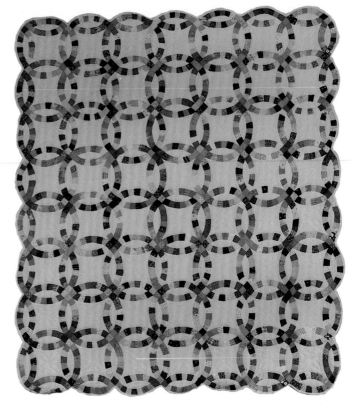

209388 - DOUBLE WEDDING RING; 88″ x 104″; multi-colored with cream background; cotton/polyester; made in 1987 in Missouri; machine pieced, hand quilted; polyester batting.   **$345.00**

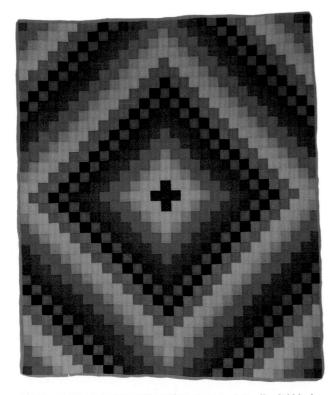

309388 - TRIP AROUND THE WORLD; 80″ x 94″; all solid blocks light to dark; cotton, cotton/poly blends; made in 1987 in Alabama; machine pieced, hand quilted; pink print lining; double quilting.   **$345.00**

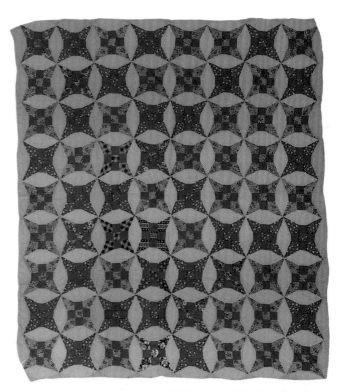

409388 - IMPROVED NINE PATCH; 71″ x 82″; blue & red; cotton; made in 1920-1930 in Missouri; hand pieced, hand quilted; unbleached muslin back; Dacron batting.   **$196.00**

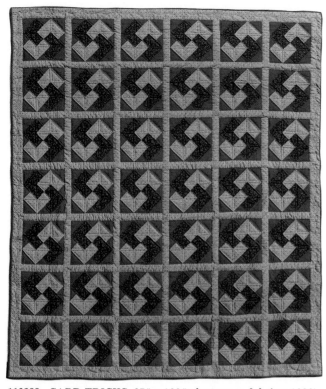

110388 - CARD TRICKS; 87″ x 100″; dusty rose & beige; 100% cotton; made in 1987; machine pieced, hand quilted; quilted ¼″ on either side of seams & border; border, sash & backing are beige background with small rose print; triangles are solid dusty rose & mauve background with dusty rose print, bound in solid rose. **$575.00**

210388 - SUNSHINE AND SHADOW CENTER DIAMOND; 92″ x 106″; Amish plain colors; 100% cotton fabrics; made in 1987 in Pennsylvania; machine pieced, hand quilted; has polyester fill; lot of quilting in black. **$662.00**

310388 - ROSE APPLIQUE; 70″ x 91″; pink, green & white; cotton; made in 1984 in Kentucky; hand appliqued; kit. **$403.00**

410388 - DOGWOOD BLOSSOMS; 77″ x 95″; pink, green, brown, yellow & white; cotton; made in 1940 in Pennsylvania; hand quilted, hand appliqued; mint condition. **$403.00**

111388 - ROYAL STAR OF VERMONT; 96″ x 106″; dusty rose prints & solids; cotton-polyester blend; made in 1987 in Missouri; machine pieced, hand quilted; white fill & white lining; has Dupont Dacron batting. **$345.00**

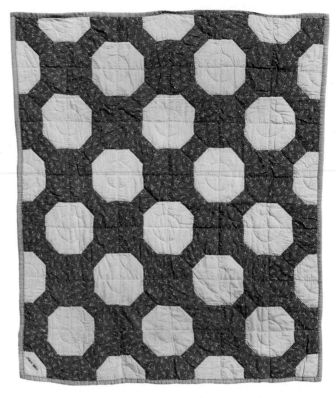

211388 - SNOWBALL; 43″ x 50″; muslin-brown print; cotton-pre-washed; made in 1986 in Kentucky; hand pieced, hand quilted; pre-washed; has close quilting by the piece with a polyester batting; hem is briar stitched. **$87.00**

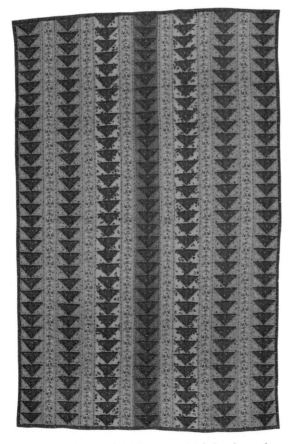

311388 - FLYING GEESE; 54″ x 79″; beige & purple; cotton-cotton/polyester; made in 1986 in California; machine pieced, hand quilted. **$403.00**

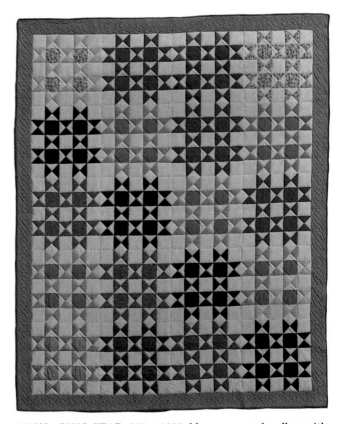

411388 - OHIO STAR; 87″ x 105″; blue, green, red, yellow with cream background & back; cotton & cotton/poly; made in 1986 in Indiana; machine pieced, hand quilted; planned color groups of Ohio Stars, especially great for rooms with antique accent; fabric pre-washed; bonded poly-batting. **$575.00**

112388 - FLYING GEESE; 76″ x 101″; rose & black are predominate colors; cotton & cotton blends; made in 1987 in Arkansas; machine pieced, hand quilted; very colorful. **$230.00**

212388 - LOG CABIN; 94″ x 113″; green & gold; polyester-cotton; made in 1986 in Illinois; machine pieced, hand quilted; traditional pattern; all new fabric. **$230.00**

312388 - LONE STAR QUILT; 96″ x 110″; lavendar; cotton & polyester & cotton; made in 1987 in Missouri; machine pieced, hand quilted; made by Mennonite women. **$317.00**

412388 - UNTITLED; 84″ x 103″; pastel blue & pink; polyester & cotton; made in 1987; machine pieced, hand quilted; quilted by piece around each seam. **$328.00**

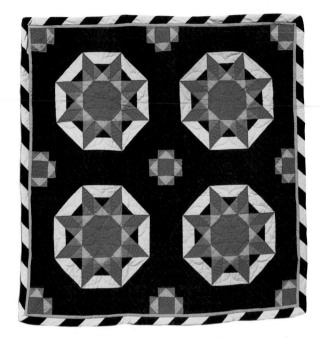

113388 - INDIA STAR; 45″ x 45″; black, red, rose, turquoise & light purple; pre-washed cotton; made in 1986 in West Virginia; machine pieced, hand quilted; sleeve for hanging on back; signed & dated. $202.00

213388 - JACOB'S LADDER; 83″ x 96″; navy & white; cotton; made in 1987 in Kentucky; machine pieced, hand quilted. $345.00

313388 - LOG CABIN; 84″ x 111″; blue; cotton/polyester; made in 1987 in Missouri; machine pieced, hand quilted; extra plump bonded polyester fill. $345.00

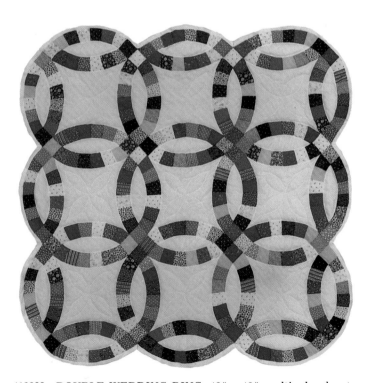

413388 - DOUBLE WEDDING RING; 42″ x 42″; multi-colored; cotton/polyester; made in 1987 in Missouri; machine pieced, hand quilted; white background. $60.00

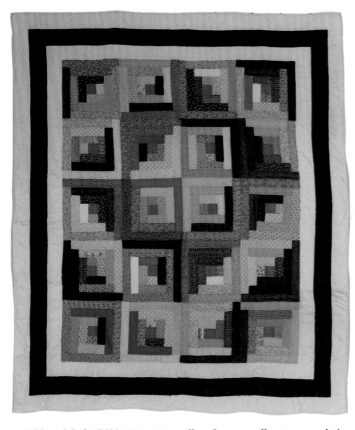

114388 - LOG CABIN; 76″ x 89″; yellow & green; all cotton; made in 1987 in Alabama; machine pieced, hand quilted; quilted on each side of seam; double batting.   **$288.00**

214388 - CHURN DASH; 63″ x 74″; multi-color; cotton; made in 1930-1940 in Missouri; machine pieced, hand quilted; Dacron batting & blue printed back; yellow sash.   **$161.00**

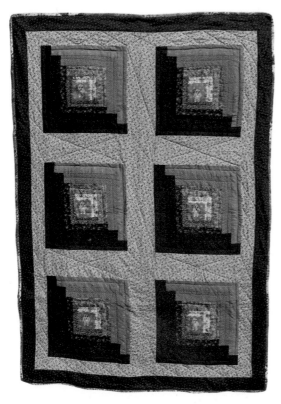

314388 - LOG CABIN; 37″ x 53″; brown & blue with gray dog in center of each cabin with light blue plaid backing; 100% cotton; made in 1987 in California; machine pieced, hand quilted; small quilt stitches.
$179.00

414388 - IMPROVED FLOWER GARDEN; 84″ x 90″; multi-print with solids; cotton/polyester; made in 1987 in Tennessee; machine pieced, hand quilted.   **$87.00**

115388 - LOG CABIN STAR; 76″ x 76″; earth tones & navy blue; cotton calico/polyester batting/muslin back; made in 1987 in New York; machine pieced, hand quilted; reproduction of older pattern; log cabin squares turned to form large center star surrounded by barn raising design. **$460.00**

215388 - ARKANSAS COON HUNTER; 96″ x 104″; beige, stripped with brown & orange; polyester & cotton blend top & bottom; made in 1986 in Arkansas; hand pieced, hand quilted, hand appliqued; poly batting. **$575.00**

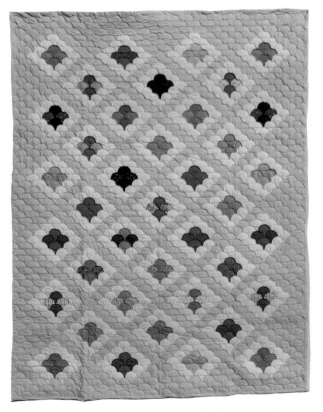

315388 - CLAM SHELL; 72″ x 90″; light blue, white & print; broadcloth polyester filling, bleached sheet lining; made in 1987 in Michigan; hand pieced, hand quilted. **$230.00**

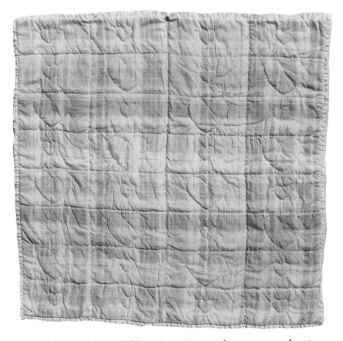

415388 - BABY HEARTS; 42″ x 43″; pastels; cottons, polyester blends; made in 1987 in Michigan; hand quilted; whole piece top with quilted hearts, white eyelet border, 100% polyester batting, bleached muslin bottom. **$52.00**

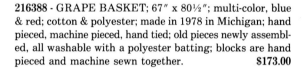

116388 - NINE PATCH; 68″ x 72″; dark blue, maroon, white & green; cotton; made in 1920; hand pieced, hand quilted; new white backing & dark blue border; interesting old fabrics; plain squares hand quilted. **$403.00**

216388 - GRAPE BASKET; 67″ x 80½″; multi-color, blue & red; cotton & polyester; made in 1978 in Michigan; hand pieced, machine pieced, hand tied; old pieces newly assembled, all washable with a polyester batting; blocks are hand pieced and machine sewn together. **$173.00**

316388 - QUILT: SPRING IS; 64″ x 64″; lavendars, blues & greens; cotton & polyblends; made in 1986 in California; hand pieced, hand quilted; quilted in the ditch; spring is lilacs, hyacinths, soft greens emerging from the winter earth. **$575.00**

416388 - OAK LEAF APPLIQUE; 74″ x 76″; solids of red, green & gold on white; cotton; made c. 1930 in Ohio; hand quilted, hand appliqued; diagonal quilting with cables quilted in borders; employs some reverse applique; bold & folksy. **$443.00**

117388 - TRIPLE IRISH CHAIN; 75″ x 101″; green & white; broadcloth; made in 1986 in Ohio; machine pieced, hand quilted; Mountain Mist polyester batting, broadcloth backing. **$345.00**

217388 - WASHINGTON CHERRY; 90″ x 108″; off-white or parchment, green & pinkish peach; poly-cotton; made in 1987 in Pennsylvania; machine pieced, hand quilted, hand appliqued; beautiful applique & embroidery; polyester fill. **$799.00**

317388 - OHIO STAR; 85½″ x 97½″; blue & white; cotton; made in 1987 in Kentucky; hand pieced, hand quilted. **$288.00**

417388 - TULIP BASKET; 65″ x 83″; blue, red, pink, green & white; cotton; made in 1930 in Pennsylvania; hand pieced, hand quilted, hand appliqued. **$385.00**

118388 - ROYAL STAR OF KANSAS; 93″ x 104″; royal blue solids & print, light blue solids & print; polyester-cotton blend, white fill & backing; made in 1987 in Missouri; machine pieced, hand quilted; plump DuPont Dacron batting. $345.00

218388 - BOWTIE; 38″ x 53″; reds, blues of light colors; cotton blends; made in 1987 in Kentucky; hand pieced, hand quilted; baby quilt made of reds & blues with a light blue lining of printed bears & small flowers; quilted by the piece; polyester batting. $87.00

318388 - FLYING BIRDS; 79″ x 85″; golds, whites & browns; cotton-cotton/polyester; made in 1985 in Ohio; machine pieced, hand quilted. $575.00

418388 - TWISTING STAR; 88″ x 103″; predominantly blue, medium green center, border piping, off-white top & backing; cotton & cotton/poly; made in 1985 in Indiana; machine pieced, hand quilted; sashing is an integral part of this pattern; fabric pre-washed; bonded poly-batting. $547.00

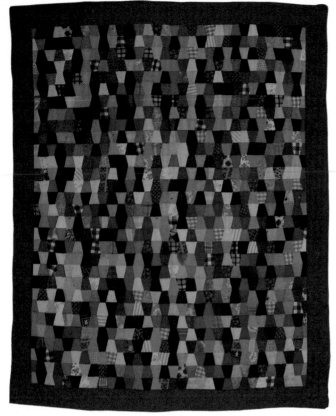

119388 - TUMBLER; 86″ x 106″; cranberry; cotton, cotton blends; made in 1987 in Arkansas; machine pieced, hand quilted; border has hearts quilted on it; very colorful.   **$230.00**

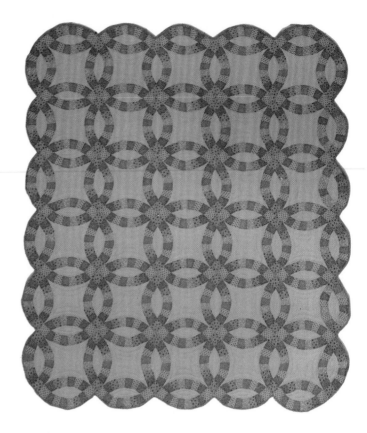

219388 - WEDDING RING; 96″ x 108″; pastels, gold; polyester-cottons; made in 1986 in Illinois; machine pieced, hand quilted. **$259.00**

319388 - LONE STAR QUILT; 96″ x 110″; lavendar; cotton & polyester & cotton; made in 1987 in Missouri; machine pieced, hand quilted; made by Mennonite women.   **$403.00**

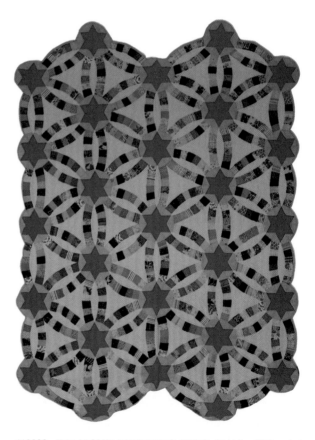

419388 - DIAMOND WEDDING RING; 81½″ x 92″; print & solid color beige, blue & rose; cotton & cotton polyester; made in 1986 in Missouri; machine pieced, hand quilted.   **$328.00**

120388 - AMISH INSPIRATION; 38″ x 38″; made in 1986 in West Virginia; machine pieced, hand quilted; each band is a different color, sleeve on back for hanging, signed & dated. **$172.50**

220388 - EAGLE; 83″ x 99″; yellow & white; cotton; made in 1987; hand quilted, hand appliqued. **$374.00**

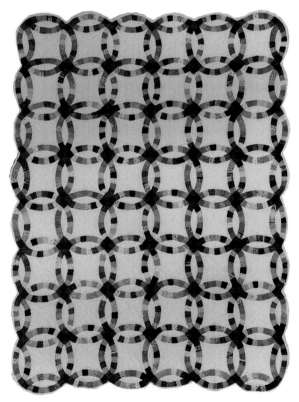

320388 - LOG CABIN; 44″ x 44″; blue/green; cotton/polyester; made in 1987 in Missouri; machine pieced, hand quilted; extra plump bonded polyester fill. **$60.00**

420388 - DOUBLE WEDDING RING; 76″ x 101″; earth tones; cotton/polyester; made in 1987 in Missouri; machine pieced, hand quilted; cream background, polyester batting. **$288.00**

121388 - LOG CABIN; 72″ x 90″; blue on blue; cotton; made in 1987 in Alabama; machine pieced, hand quilted; quilted on each side of seam; light blue lining. $288.00

221388 - DAHLIA; 96″ x 110″; dusty blue/navy; 50/50 cotton/poly; made in 1987 in Missouri; machine pieced, hand quilted; Dacron batting; off-white background & back. $403.00

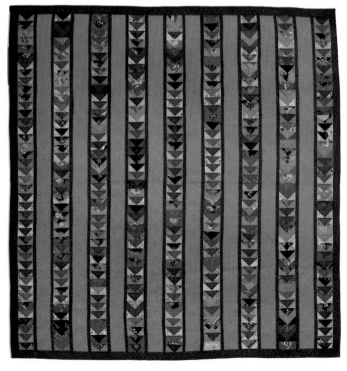

321388 - FLOCKS OF BIRDS; 91″ x 93″; golds & browns; cotton-cotton/polyester; made in 1984 in Ohio; machine pieced, hand quilted. $403.00

421388 - LONE STAR; 84″ x 89″; rainbow colors; all cotton; made in 1987 in Indiana; hand pieced, machine quilted; Mountain Mist batting, pale yellow border. $144.00

122388 - LONE STAR; 80″ x 90″; browns; cotton/polyester blends, muslin; made in 1987 in South Carolina; machine pieced, machine quilted; made from 512 diamonds of brown & brown prints with 2 borders. **$288.00**

222388 - BROKEN STAR; 72″ x 85″; mixed colors; cotton; made in 1945 in Kentucky; hand pieced, hand quilted; mixed color quilt with a mixture of colored prints making up the star. **$299.00**

322388 - MARINER'S COMPASS MEDALLION "CARDINAL POINTS"; 88″ x 104″; brown, rose & turquoise; 100% cottons; made in 1986 in Arkansas; hand pieced, hand quilted; designed so that triangles in each border were same size. **$1,380.00**

422388 - CROSSROADS; 76″ x 92″; peach with calico background; cotton & calico; made in 1987 in Indiana; hand pieced, hand quilted; quilt is alive with colors surrounded by applique flowers. **$288.00**

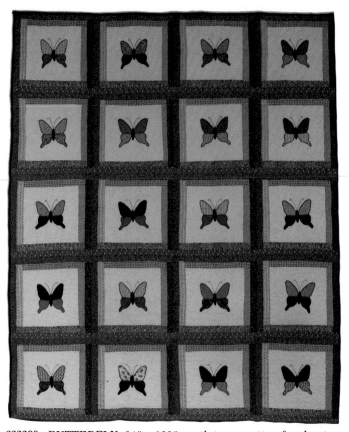

123388 - TULIP; 70″ x 92″; poly-cotton; made in 1986 in Texas; hand pieced, hand quilted, hand appliqued on to off-white poly-cotton; bordered with dark rose & brown; free flowing hand quilting on lap; no frame; washable with care. **$403.00**

223388 - BUTTERFLY; 84″ x 102″; earth tones; cotton & polyester; made in 1985 in Indiana; machine quilted, machine appliqued; all new material, Mountain Mist batting, machine quilted in beautiful design. **$144.00**

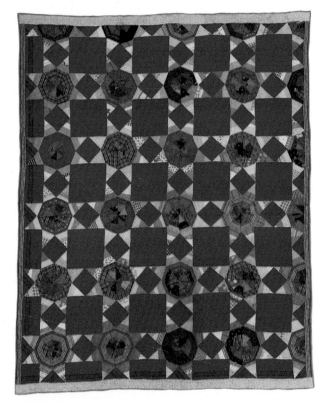

323388 - 8 POINT STAR; 67″ x 81″; red & blue; cotton; made in 1930 in Kentucky; hand pieced, hand quilted; very typical of quilts from this time period; basically made up of red & blue calico with other colors blending. **$299.00**

423388 - DAWN OVER AN AMISH FARM; 24″ x 24″; shimmering pastels in stars, cobalt blue border, bound with light turquoise; made in 1987 in 100% cotton, some polished cotton & cotton sateen; machine pieced, hand quilted; border is quilted with a continuous cable pattern, pre-washed fabrics, cotton batting, signed & dated, exhibited in Missouri Art Gallery. **$115.00**

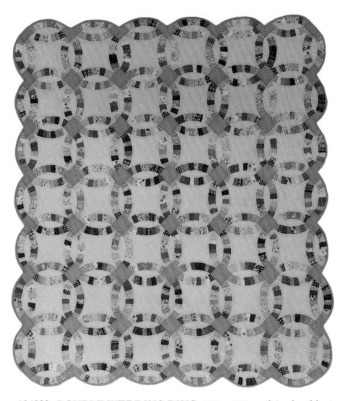

124388 - DOUBLE WEDDING RING; 72″ x 83″; multi-color (blue); cotton/polyester blend & muslin; made in 1987 in South Carolina; machine pieced, hand quilted. **$575.00**

224388 - LOG CABIN; 70″ x 96″; blues & tans; top is 100% pre-washed cotton, back is blend muslin; made in 1987 in Pennsylvania; machine pieced, hand quilted; blue binding, beige whole piece backing. **$345.00**

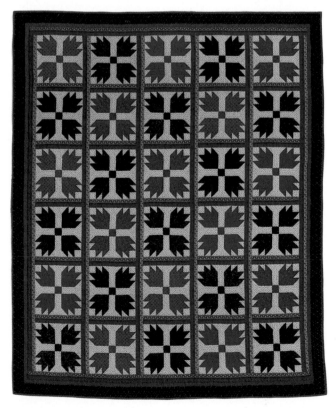

324388 - TULIPS, LOTS OF TULIPS; 99″ x 108″; green, 2 shades of pink, off-white; 100% cotton; made in 1987 in Wisconsin; hand quilted, hand appliqued. **$569.00**

424388 - BEAR'S PAW; 76″ x 91″; red, blues, off-white background; 100% cotton; made in 1986 in Arkansas; machine pieced, hand quilted; uses a quilting design that does not outline the pattern but stands on its own. **$345.00**

125388 - LOVER'S KNOT; 56″ x 56″; dark blue, pinks, light blue; 100% pre-washed cotton top, mauve blend backing; made in 1987 in Pennsylvania; machine pieced, hand quilted; dark blue print, pink print & pink solid, blue & white strips make up the interlocking lover's knot pattern, pink solid & dark blue print borders, dark blue print binding, mauve solid piece backing, blends with pinks.
$173.00

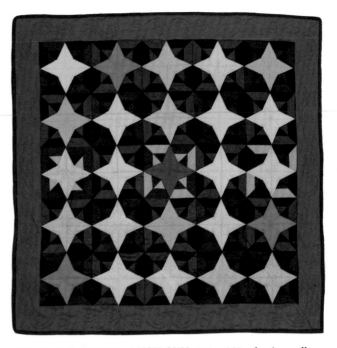

225388 - MIDNIGHT AMISH SKY; 36″ x 36″; glowing yellows in stars, sage, forest & jade green background with a touch of light turquoise, royal blue sateen border; 100% cotton & cotton sateen; made in 1987 in Missouri; hand pieced, machine pieced, hand quilted; cotton batting, exhibited in Missouri Art Gallery, signed & dated.
$156.00

325388 - THE STAR; 76″ x 90″; blue & white with white background; cotton blend; made in 1987 in Indiana; hand pieced, hand quilted.
$288.00

425388 - SPIDER WEB; 72″ x 86″; green printed with blue; cotton; made in 1937 in New England; hand pieced, hand quilted; green, pink & blue spider webs on muslin; green printed backing.
$345.00

126388 - BLOCK; 65½″ x 84″; mixed colors; cotton blends; made in 1945 in Tennessee; hand pieced, hand quilted; made of 2″ blocks in assorted light to medium prints, some fading on back, quilted by the piece. **$144.00**

226388 - SOUTHERN BELL; 70″ x 84″; blue & mauve; cotton blends on muslin; made in 1986 in South Carolina; hand appliqued, hand quilted; 2 blue & 2 mauve Southern Bells. **$593.00**

326388 - SUNBONNET GIRL; 76″ x 85″; gold & ecru; all cotton; made in 1985 in Indiana; machine quilted, hand appliqued; Mountain Mist batting. **$144.00**

426388 - "BEAR PAW" A.K.A. "DUCK'S FOOT IN THE MUD"; 94″ x 112″; dusty rose, blue & cream; 100% cotton; made in 1987 in Wisconsin; hand pieced, machine pieced, hand quilted; shades of blue & dusty rose flowers, green leaves, dark purple background with dusty rose pin dot strips & claws; cream accent. **$420.00**